HOMARUS GAMMARUS

Homarus Gammarus

THE EUROPEAN LOBSTER IN ATLANTIC WATERS

Rafeal Mechlore

Spectra Enterprise

Contents

INDEX

INTRODUCTION

The huge span of the Atlantic Sea, with its flows, tides, and various biological systems, harbors a heap of marine life. Inside this watery domain, one notable scavanger sticks out — the European Lobster, deductively known as Homarus gammarus. Prestigious for its tasty taste and particular appearance, the European Lobster assumes a significant environmental part in the Atlantic Waters, adding to the perplexing equilibrium of marine biological systems. This investigation dives into the life, science, circulation, and meaning of Homarus gammarus, disentangling the story of this regarded species in the immense and dynamic Atlantic Waters.

1. **Ordered Characterization: Uncovering the Personality of Homarus Gammarus**

   1.1 The Realm of Homarus:

   Homarus gammarus, an individual from the phylum Arthropoda, class Malacostraca, and request Decapoda, has a place with the family Nephropidae. The ordered excursion starts with an investigation of its characterization, uncovering the developmental heredity that puts the European Lobster inside the assorted realm of life.

   1.2 Exploring the Lobster Genealogy:

   Inside the family Nephropidae, the European Lobster imparts connection to different lobsters, separating itself through remarkable morphological and hereditary elements. Understanding the ordered place of Homarus gammarus establishes the groundwork for unwinding its science, conduct, and environmental associations.

2. **Science and Life Cycle: The Many-sided Dance of Development and Proliferation**

   2.1 Morphology and Life structures:

   The European Lobster displays a captivating cluster of morphological transformations, from its vigorous exoskeleton and strong paws to the perplexing design of its gills and tangible limbs. Investigating the life systems of Homarus gammarus gives bits of knowledge into its methods for surviving and natural specialty.

2.2 Life Cycle Stages:

The existence pattern of Homarus gammarus is an enrapturing adventure of development and change. From the tiny hatchlings incubating from eggs to the experienced grown-ups watching the seabed, every life stage adds to the strength and propagation of the species. Understanding these stages discloses the ensemble of life in Atlantic Waters.

3. **Appropriation and Living space: Exploring the Atlantic Void**

   3.1 Geographic Reach:

   Homarus gammarus is an inhabitant of the Atlantic Sea, with its reach stretching out from the subarctic waters of the North Atlantic to the calm environments of the Mediterranean Ocean. The investigation of its geographic reach reveals the versatility of this species to assorted natural circumstances.

   3.2 Natural surroundings Inclinations:

   Inside the tremendousness of the Atlantic Waters, the European Lobster shows particular natural surroundings inclinations. Rough substrates, kelp backwoods, and sandy bottoms act as favored districts for safe house and scavenging. Analyzing the particular environment prerequisites of Homarus gammarus gives experiences into the difficulties and open doors it faces as its continued looking for endurance.

4. **Nature and Social Transformations: The Puzzling Way of life of Homarus Gammarus**

   4.1 Natural Collaborations:

   As a cornerstone animal groups in marine environments, Homarus gammarus participates in complex natural cooperations. From its job as a hunter controlling invertebrate populaces to filling in as prey for bigger marine hunters, the European Lobster meshes itself into the complex snare of Atlantic Waters biology.

   4.2 Social Variations:

   The social collection of Homarus gammarus includes a different arrangement of transformations. From tunneling ways of behaving for safe house to perplexing romance ceremonies and regional presentations, the European Lobster's ways of behaving are finely tuned to its current circumstance. Inspecting these transformations gives a window into the systems utilized for endurance and propagation.

5. **Monetary Importance and Human Associations: Homarus Gammarus in Human Culture**

5.1 Culinary Joys:

Homarus gammarus holds a unique spot in human culture, especially in culinary practices. Known for its delicious meat and rich flavor, the European Lobster graces the tables of connoisseur cafés and shoreline feasts. The investigation of its monetary importance in the culinary world discloses the social and gastronomic worth put on this shellfish.

5.2 Fisheries and Business Significance:

Past its allure on supper plates, the European Lobster assumes a focal part in business fisheries. With a set of experiences established in conventional fishing rehearses, lobster fisheries have developed into a worldwide industry. Inspecting the business significance reveals insight into the financial elements and difficulties looked by the individuals who rely upon lobster harvests for their livelihoods.

6. **Authentic Point of view: Homarus Gammarus in the Chronicles of Fisheries**

6.1 Early Reaps and Conventional Practices:

The verifiable point of view of Homarus gammarus follows back to the beginning of human cooperation with marine assets. Customary gathering techniques, including lobster pots and traps, uncover the central practices that formed the connection among networks and lobster populaces.

6.2 Evolving Tides: Difficulties and Preservation Endeavors:

Throughout the long term, the European Lobster has confronted difficulties, for example, overfishing, living space debasement, and changes in ecological circumstances. The story of changing tides investigates the advancement of preservation endeavors, administrative measures, and local area drives pointed toward guaranteeing the reasonable administration of lobster populaces.

7. **Protection Status and Difficulties: Shielding the European Lobster**

7.1 Preservation Status:

Surveying the preservation status of Homarus gammarus includes assessing populace patterns, living space wellbeing, and the effect of human exercises. The assessment of preservation status gives a preview of the difficulties looked by European Lobster populaces and illuminates designated mediations for their insurance.

7.2 Dangers to Endurance:

Various dangers loom over the endurance of Homarus gammarus, going from overfishing and environment annihilation to environmental change and contamination. Distinguishing and understanding these dangers is significant for figuring out powerful preservation procedures that address the underlying drivers of populace decline.

8. **Environmental Change Effects: Homarus Gammarus in a Changing Sea**

8.1 Maritime Movements:

The impact of environmental change on the Atlantic Waters has significant ramifications for Homarus gammarus. Changes in ocean temperature, sea fermentation, and adjusted flows influence the dissemination, conduct, and physiology of the European Lobster. Inspecting the environmental change influences gives a brief look into the difficulties presented by a quickly changing maritime climate.

8.2 Transformations and Flexibility:

Homarus gammarus, in the same way as other marine species, shows variations to adapt to the evolving conditions. Understanding the systems of variation and the versatility of the European Lobster offers expect its proceeded with endurance notwithstanding environment related difficulties.

9. **Research Strategies and Innovative Headways: Revealing Lobster Secrets**

9.1 Customary Strategies:

The investigation of Homarus gammarus has been formed by conventional examination techniques, including field overviews, example assortments, and natural perceptions. These central methodologies laid the basis for figuring out lobster science and environment.

9.2 Mechanical Developments:

Progressions in innovation have impelled lobster examination into another time. From submerged robots and satellite following to hereditary examinations and bioinformatics, innovation opens new outskirts for disentangling the secrets of Homarus gammarus. The incorporation of these developments improves the accuracy and extent of lobster studies.

10. **Hydroponics Potential: Developing Homarus Gammarus for What's in store**

10.1 Maintainable Hydroponics Practices:

In light of the difficulties looked by wild lobster populaces, hydroponics arises as a likely road for supporting Homarus gammarus. Economical hydroponics works on, including incubator tasks, coastal frameworks, and in-water nooks, offer a promising pathway to guarantee the proceeded with accessibility of European Lobster while limiting effects on wild populaces.

10.2 Financial and Ecological Effects:

The investigation of hydroponics potential includes evaluating the monetary suitability and natural manageability of development rehearses. Adjusting the requests of business creation with the protection of wild stocks requires cautious thought of the environmental, social, and financial components of lobster hydroponics.

1. Overview of the European Lobster (Homarus gammarus)

The European Lobster, deductively known as Homarus gammarus, remains as an image of the rich marine biodiversity occupying the beach front waters of the North Atlantic. This scavanger, prestigious for its culinary allure and natural importance, has charmed the consideration of researchers, anglers, and fans the same. In this thorough outline, we dive into the multi-layered parts of Homarus gammarus, investigating its scientific categorization, science, life cycle, dispersion, territory inclinations, natural communications, monetary significance, verifiable setting, protection status, and the difficulties and open doors it faces in the evolving oceans.

1. **Scientific categorization and Characterization: Disclosing the Personality of Homarus gammarus**

   1.1 Phylogenetic Setting:

   Homarus gammarus has a place with the different phylum Arthropoda, class Malacostraca, and request Decapoda. Its ordered excursion is described by a complicated trap of connections inside the family Nephropidae, putting it among the regarded lobsters in the marine domain. Understanding the phylogenetic setting lays the preparation for investigating the perplexing highlights that characterize this species.

   1.2 Key Ordered Qualities:

   The scientific classification of Homarus gammarus includes the recognizable proof of key attributes that recognize it from other marine life forms. From its particular morphology to hereditary markers, researchers utilize a scope of standards to disentangle the ordered complexities of this notorious scavanger.

2. **Science and Morphology: Disentangling the Life structures of Homarus gammarus**

   2.1 Outer Morphology:

   The outer morphology of Homarus gammarus exhibits an exceptional cluster of highlights intended for endurance in the marine climate. From its defensive exoskeleton and chelae to tangible recieving wires, a more critical glance at the lobster's outer life structures gives experiences into its transformations and natural jobs.

   2.2 Inner Life systems:

   Past the external shell, the inner life structures of Homarus gammarus uncovers the complexities of its physiological frameworks. The stomach related, circulatory, and regenerative frameworks assume essential parts in the existence cycles of this shellfish. Investigating the interior life systems reveals insight into the instruments that support its presence.

3. **Life Cycle Stages: The Orchestra of Development and Change**

3.1 Larval Turn of events:

The existence pattern of Homarus gammarus unfurls in a progression of stages, starting with the minute hatchlings bring forth from eggs. These hatchlings go through an intriguing excursion of improvement, exploring the difficulties of the marine climate. Understanding larval improvement is pivotal for grasping the elements of lobster populaces.

3.2 Adolescent and Grown-up Stages:

As hatchlings transform into adolescents and in the end into grown-ups, every life stage brings one of a kind difficulties and open doors. From tracking down reasonable environments to exploring conceptive ways of behaving, the changes in the existence pattern of Homarus gammarus add to the versatility and manageability of populaces.

4. **Appropriation and Territory Inclinations: Homarus gammarus in Atlantic Waters**

4.1 Geographic Reach:

Homarus gammarus is an occupant of the huge Atlantic Sea, with its geographic reach crossing from the subarctic waters of the North Atlantic to the mild environments of the Mediterranean Ocean. Inspecting the dispersion examples of this species gives experiences into its flexibility to assorted maritime circumstances.

4.2 Environment Inclinations:

Inside the broad Atlantic Waters, the European Lobster shows explicit territory inclinations. Rough substrates, kelp woods, and protected regions act as vital territories for taking care of, shedding, and proliferation. Examining these inclinations uncovers the complex connection between Homarus gammarus and its picked surroundings.

5. **Biological Communications: Homarus gammarus in the Marine Environment**

5.1 Cornerstone Species Status:

Homarus gammarus expects the job of a cornerstone animal types in marine environments, impacting the overflow and conduct of different life forms. As a hunter, it manages the populaces of spineless creatures, adding to the biological equilibrium. The cornerstone status of the European Lobster highlights its importance in keeping up with the soundness of seaside environments.

5.2 Predation and Prey Elements:

The natural cooperations of Homarus gammarus stretch out to its job as both hunter and prey. From rummaging on benthic organic entities to filling in as a food hotspot for bigger marine hunters, the lobster takes part in powerful connections inside the multifaceted food web of Atlantic Waters.

6. **Monetary Significance: Homarus gammarus in Fisheries and Hydroponics**

6.1 Conventional Fisheries:

The financial significance of Homarus gammarus is well established in conventional fisheries that have molded beach front networks for a really long time. Lobster fisheries, driven by the interest for this valued shellfish, have added to the jobs and social character of areas along the Atlantic coast.

6.2 Culinary Importance:

The culinary allure of Homarus gammarus expands its financial significance past fishing networks. Lobsters are pursued for their delicious meat and particular flavor, making them a delicacy in worldwide culinary customs. The investigation of their culinary importance dives into the market elements and buyer inclinations related with this marine fortune.

7. **Verifiable Viewpoint: Advancement of Homarus gammarus Fisheries**

7.1 Early Gathers and Customary Practices:

The verifiable viewpoint of Homarus gammarus follows back to the early communications between human social orders and marine assets. Customary collecting strategies, for example, lobster pots and traps, uncover the social and mechanical advancement of lobster fisheries. Analyzing early collects gives experiences into the reasonable practices utilized by authentic networks.

7.2 Industrialization and Globalization:

With the coming of industrialization and globalization, the elements of lobster fisheries went through huge changes. Expanded request, mechanical progressions, and extended markets molded the direction of the business. Investigating the authentic development of lobster fisheries divulges the perplexing transaction between cultural requests and marine asset the board.

8. **Preservation Status and Difficulties: Protecting Homarus gammarus Populaces**

8.1 Populace Appraisals:

Surveying the preservation status of Homarus gammarus includes methodical populace evaluations. Researchers utilize different strategies, including submerged reviews, mark-recover studies, and hereditary investigations, to check the wellbeing and wealth of lobster populaces. The aftereffects of these appraisals structure the reason for informed protection techniques.

8.2 Anthropogenic Dangers:

Regardless of its flexibility, Homarus gammarus faces a range of anthropogenic dangers that imperil its populaces. Overfishing, environment annihilation, contamination, and environmental change present imposing difficulties to the prosperity of this species. Distinguishing and understanding these dangers are significant for planning successful protection measures.

9. **Environmental Change Effects: Homarus gammarus in a Changing Sea**

9.1 Maritime Changes:

The impact of environmental change on the Atlantic Waters has flowing consequences for Homarus gammarus. Changes in ocean temperature, sea fermentation, and modifications in flow designs influence the dissemination, conduct, and physiology of lobsters. Exploring the environmental change influences gives a focal point into the difficulties presented by a quickly changing maritime climate.

9.2 Transformations and Strength:

Homarus gammarus, in the same way as other marine species, shows transformations to adapt to the changing circumstances actuated by environmental change. Understanding the components of transformation and the strength of the European Lobster offers experiences into its ability to explore the difficulties presented by a moving environment.

10. **Research Strategies and Mechanical Progressions: Unwinding Lobster Secrets**

10.1 Conventional Techniques:

The investigation of Homarus gammarus has advanced through customary examination techniques, including field perceptions, example assortments, and biological studies. These basic methodologies laid the basis for grasping lobster science, conduct, and environmental jobs.

10.2 Mechanical Advancements:

Ongoing many years have seen a transformation in lobster research through mechanical headways. From submerged robots and satellite following to hereditary examinations and bioinformatics, innovation upgrades the accuracy and extent of lobster review. The mix of these advancements opens new boondocks for unwinding the secrets of Homarus gammarus.

11. **Hydroponics Potential: Developing Homarus gammarus for Economical Fates**

11.1 Maintainable Hydroponics Practices:

In light of the difficulties looked by wild lobster populaces, hydroponics arises as a possible road for supporting Homarus gammarus. Economical hydroponics works on, including incubator tasks, coastal frameworks, and in-water nooks, offer a promising pathway to guarantee the proceeded with accessibility of European Lobster while limiting effects on wild populaces.

11.2 Monetary and Ecological Effects:

The investigation of hydroponics potential includes surveying the monetary practicality and natural manageability of development rehearses. Adjusting the requests of business creation with the preservation of wild stocks requires cautious thought of the environmental, social, and monetary components of lobster hydroponics.

B. Significance of studying the species in Atlantic Waters

The Atlantic Sea, with its tremendous field and dynamic biological systems, fills in as a cauldron of life, facilitating a bunch of animal groups that add to the unpredictable embroidery of marine biodiversity. Understanding the meaning of concentrating on species in Atlantic Waters is fundamental for unwinding the natural, financial, and social complexities that characterize this broad maritime domain. This complete investigation digs into the complex significance of concentrating on the assorted exhibit of species occupying the Atlantic, looking at their jobs in environmental equilibrium, the effect on human social orders, the social importance, and the ramifications for preservation and reasonable asset the executives.

1. **Biodiversity and Natural Equilibrium: Watchmen of Atlantic Biological systems**

   1.1 Cornerstone Species and Biodiversity:

   The species possessing Atlantic Waters assume critical parts as cornerstone species, applying a lopsided effect on the design and capability of their individual environments. Understanding the biodiversity of Atlantic species gives bits of knowledge into the sensitive equilibrium that supports the wellbeing and strength of marine conditions.

   1.2 Trophic Cooperations and Food Networks:

   Species in Atlantic Waters participate in complex trophic cooperations, shaping complicated food networks that oversee energy stream and supplement cycling. Concentrating on these connections uncovers the conditions and connections among species, revealing insight into the flowing impacts that aggravations or changes in populace elements can have on whole environments.

2. **Financial Significance: Marine Assets as Monetary Motors**

   2.1 Fisheries and Worldwide Economy:

   Atlantic Waters are a worldwide focal point for fisheries, supporting energetic enterprises that contribute essentially to the worldwide economy. The investigation of species in these waters is vital for fisheries the executives, surveying stocks, and understanding the financial elements that connect marine assets to vocations and markets around the world.

   2.2 Hydroponics and Economical Creation:

   Species concentrated on in Atlantic Waters frequently track down applications in hydroponics, offering open doors for supportable and controlled creation. Investigating the hydroponics capability of different species adds to food security, monetary broadening, and diminished strain on wild populaces, encouraging a harmony between asset usage and preservation.

3. **Social Importance: Species as Symbols of Character and Custom**

   3.1 Culinary Practices and Gastronomic Joys:

   Numerous species in Atlantic Waters hold social importance, particularly with regards to culinary practices. Concentrating on the gastronomic inclinations and social practices related with these species uncovers the well established associations among networks and the marine assets that support them.

   3.2 Famous Species and Social Personality:

   Certain species act as symbols of social personality, encapsulating the soul of waterfront networks. From fables to festivities, the investigation of these species gives a window into the social stories and customs that have developed over ages, molding the personality of networks along the Atlantic coast.

4. **Preservation and Supportable Asset The executives: Saving the Maritime Legacy**

   4.1 Compromised Species and Preservation Needs:

   The investigation of species in Atlantic Waters incorporates evaluating the preservation status of helpless and jeopardized populaces. Recognizing compromised species and understanding the elements adding to their downfall are fundamental stages in planning powerful protection systems and asset the executives plans.

   4.2 Environment Based Administration:

   Species act as signs of environment wellbeing, and their review is indispensable to the advancement of biological system based administration methodologies. Such methodologies think about the interconnections between species, environments, and human exercises, intending to guarantee the manageability of Atlantic biological systems for people in the future.

5. **Environmental Change Flexibility: Figuring out Species in a Changing Climate**

   5.1 Environmental Change Effects on Species:

   The investigation of species in Atlantic Waters gives pivotal experiences into the effects of environmental change. Changes in temperature, sea fermentation, and adjusted sea flows influence the appropriation, conduct, and physiology of species. Understanding these effects is fundamental for anticipating and relieving the environmental outcomes of an evolving environment.

   5.2 Versatile Procedures and Strength:

   Species show a scope of versatile techniques to adapt to ecological changes. Concentrating on these systems gives important data to surveying the versatility of species notwithstanding environmental change. Bits of knowledge into versatile components illuminate preservation endeavors and techniques for dealing with the effects of a warming sea.

6. **Logical Request and Revelations: Propelling Information on Atlantic Life**

6.1 Investigation and Scientific categorization:

The investigation of species in Atlantic Waters adds to the progression of scientific categorization and our comprehension of the variety of life. New species keep on being found, and progressing ordered research refines our arrangement frameworks, improving our grip of the intricacy of Atlantic biological systems.

6.2 Conduct Biology and Biotic Cooperations:

Logical investigation into the way of behaving and environment of species gives a more profound comprehension of their jobs in the biological system. From transient examples to multifaceted biotic connections, concentrating on species improves our insight into the basic cycles that shape the working of Atlantic marine conditions.

7. **Biotic Network: Connections Between Atlantic Waters and Worldwide Seas**

7.1 Movement and Network:

Numerous species in Atlantic Waters take part in transitory examples that stretch out past local limits. Understanding these movement courses and examples lays out the network between Atlantic environments and other maritime districts. This biotic availability is significant for thorough marine protection and the executives endeavors.

7.2 Worldwide Ramifications of Atlantic Species:

The investigation of Atlantic species has worldwide ramifications, as the wellbeing and elements of these biological systems impact the more extensive maritime climate. Changes in species populaces, circulation, and conduct in Atlantic Waters can have flowing impacts on marine environments around the world, underlining the interconnected idea of the planet's seas.

8. **Ecological Schooling and Mindfulness: Encouraging Sea Education**

8.1 Effort and Training Drives:

The investigation of species in Atlantic Waters fills in as an establishment for ecological schooling and effort drives. By cultivating sea proficiency, these endeavors engage networks to comprehend the significance of marine protection, practical asset use, and the job people play in safeguarding the wellbeing of the seas.

8.2 Resident Science and Participatory Exploration:

Drawing in the general population in the investigation of species advances resident science and participatory examination. Including people group in information assortment, observing, and protection drives contributes significant data as well as improves public mindfulness and a feeling of stewardship for Atlantic marine conditions.

9. **Moral Contemplations: Adjusting Use and Protection**

9.1 Moral Reaping Practices:

The investigation of species in Atlantic Waters raises moral contemplations with respect to gathering rehearses. Adjusting the use of marine assets for monetary and culinary purposes with the protection of weak populaces requires moral independent direction and supportable administration rehearses.

9.2 Native Information and Moral Coordinated effort:

Native people group frequently have customary information about species and biological systems. Moral cooperation with these networks recognizes the significance of native viewpoints in protection and asset the executives, encouraging a comprehensive methodology that coordinates logical information with nearby insight.

10. **Difficulties and Future Headings: Exploring Complex Waters**

10.1 Beating Information Holes:

Notwithstanding progresses in sea life science, huge information holes endure in how we might interpret species in Atlantic Waters. Tending to these holes requires coordinated endeavors in research financing, joint effort, and the improvement of creative strategies to upgrade information assortment and examination.

10.2 Coordinating Interdisciplinary Methodologies:

The intricacy of Atlantic marine environments requires interdisciplinary ways to deal with concentrate on species exhaustively. Joint efforts between scholars, oceanographers, climatologists, and social researchers can give a more comprehensive comprehension of the multifaceted connections among species and their surroundings.

C. Objectives of the book

The targets of this book stretch out past a simple investigation of the species in Atlantic Waters; they embody a thorough undertaking to disentangle the intricacies of marine biological systems, human communications, and the sensitive equilibrium that supports life in the tremendous Atlantic Sea. Through a complex focal point, the book looks to accomplish a few general goals that add to our aggregate comprehension of the importance, difficulties, and potential open doors inborn in concentrating on the species possessing this broad and dynamic sea space.

1. **Disclosing Ordered Secrets: Grasping the Character of Atlantic Species**

   1.1 Ordered Grouping and Distinguishing proof

   One essential goal of this book is to dive into the ordered secrets of the species in Atlantic Waters. By disentangling the unpredictable trap of characterization, perusers will acquire bits of knowledge into the developmental connections, morphological variations, and hereditary qualifications that characterize every species. An exhaustive comprehension of ordered personality frames the establishment for ensuing investigations into the science, nature, and preservation of these marine living beings.

1.2 Investigating Variety:

Variety is a sign of Atlantic Waters, and this book expects to exhibit the wealth of species that possess these marine conditions. From tiny creatures to famous megafauna, the investigation of ordered variety serves not exclusively to list the occupants of Atlantic Waters yet additionally to feature the interconnectedness and relationship of assorted life structures in the maritime environment.

2. **Disentangling Environmental Elements: Translating the Communications Inside Atlantic Biological systems**

2.1 Biological Comprehension and Interconnectedness

The book tries to unwind the natural elements that administer Atlantic Waters. By inspecting trophic cooperations, food networks, and the jobs of species as cornerstone organic entities, perusers will acquire a more profound appreciation for the multifaceted equilibrium that supports the wellbeing and flexibility of marine biological systems. Understanding these elements is vital for powerful preservation and practical asset the board.

2.2 Biotic Network:

The goal reaches out to investigating the biotic network that joins Atlantic environments with worldwide seas. Relocation designs, sea flows, and the transient ways of behaving of species rise above provincial limits. By fathoming these examples, the book expects to reveal insight into the interconnected idea of Atlantic Waters and their effect on more extensive marine conditions.

3. **Assessing Monetary Importance: Evaluating the Effect on Human Social orders**

3.1 Financial Significance and Fisheries The board

A basic target of the book is to assess the monetary meaning of species in Atlantic Waters. By analyzing the job of marine assets in fisheries and hydroponics, perusers will acquire bits of knowledge into the monetary motors that drive waterfront networks and add to the worldwide economy. Understanding the monetary elements is fundamental for feasible fisheries the executives and the impartial usage of marine assets.

3.2 Culinary and Social Importance:

Past monetary worth, the book looks to investigate the culinary and social meaning of species in Atlantic Waters. Culinary customs, gastronomic joys, and the social personality related with specific species add to the rich woven artwork of waterfront networks. By diving into these viewpoints, the book plans to feature the interlaced connections between human social orders and the marine climate.

4. **Encouraging Preservation Mindfulness: Focusing on the Soundness of Atlantic Environments**

4.1 Preservation Needs and Danger Appraisal

The book plans to cultivate protection mindfulness by focusing on the well-being of Atlantic environments. Evaluating the protection status of weak species, recognizing dangers, and understanding the ramifications of human exercises on marine conditions are focal goals. The objective is to give perusers the information expected to advocate for and effectively take part in preservation endeavors.

4.2 Economical Asset The executives:

Supplementing protection mindfulness, the book looks to advance economical asset the board rehearses. By looking at fruitful contextual investigations, creative methodologies, and examples gained from protection drives, perusers can acquire bits of knowledge into compelling techniques for offsetting human requirements with the safeguarding of Atlantic marine biodiversity.

5. **Tending to Environmental Change Effects: Adjusting to a Changing Maritime Climate**

5.1 Environmental Change Strength and Versatile Methodologies

Given the rising effect of environmental change on maritime conditions, the book expects to address the difficulties and potential open doors related with a changing Atlantic Sea. Figuring out the effects on species, their versatile procedures, and the flexibility of marine environments despite environment related stressors are key goals. The objective is to enable perusers with information to add to environment strong marine preservation endeavors.

5.2 Worldwide Ramifications and Cooperative Arrangements:

The book stretches out its targets to consider the worldwide ramifications of environmental change on Atlantic Waters. By investigating cooperative arrangements, global participation, and interdisciplinary methodologies, perusers will acquire experiences into how aggregate activity can address the difficulties presented by a warming sea and moving natural circumstances.

6. **Progressing Logical Request: Adding to Sea life Science and Exploration**

6.1 Logical Headways and Mechanical Developments

An essential goal of the book is to add to logical request by propelling comprehension we might interpret species in Atlantic Waters. Investigating mechanical advancements, ongoing examination techniques, and interdisciplinary methodologies, the book plans to grandstand the state of the art commitments that push sea life science forward. Thusly, it urges perusers to draw in with progressing research and possibly add to the field.

6.2 Resident Science and Public Commitment:

Perceiving the significance of public commitment to logical undertakings, the book means to advance resident science drives. By exhibiting instances of participatory examination, local area based checking, and the job of residents in contributing significant information, the book urges perusers to take part in logical investigation and preservation endeavors effectively.

7. **Supporting Ecological Schooling: Advancing Sea Education for All**

7.1 Ecological Schooling Drives and Effort

The book looks to sustain natural training by advancing sea education. Through instructive drives, outreach programs, and the spread of information, the goal is to engage people, networks, and instructive organizations with the comprehension expected to become educated stewards regarding Atlantic Waters. This is pivotal for cultivating a feeling of obligation and manageability.

7.2 Moral Contemplations and Native Information:

Moral contemplations, including capable gathering rehearses and the incorporation of native information, structure an essential piece of the book's goals. By looking at the moral components of species study and protection, the book means to impart a feeling of moral obligation in perusers, empowering them to think about the more extensive ramifications of their communications with marine conditions.

8. **Difficulties and Future Bearings: Diagramming a Course for Far reaching Getting it**

8.1 Conquering Information Holes and Systemic Difficulties

Recognizing the difficulties innate in concentrating on species in Atlantic Waters, the book plans to address information holes and systemic difficulties. By examining momentum impediments, proposing possible arrangements, and empowering further exploration, the book looks to diagram a course for future examinations that can add to a more extensive comprehension of Atlantic marine biological systems.

8.2 Incorporating Interdisciplinary Methodologies:

The book highlights the significance of coordinating interdisciplinary ways to deal with concentrate on species extensively. By encouraging joint efforts between researchers, policymakers, networks, and different partners, the goal is to advance an all encompassing comprehension that rises above disciplinary limits, cultivating a more nuanced and interconnected viewpoint.

Chapter 1

Taxonomy, Biology, And Life Cycle

Scientific classification, the study of ordering and naming living creatures, is a major mainstay of science. It gives an orderly structure to coordinating the huge range of life on The planet, permitting researchers to classify and grasp the connections between various species. This grouping framework fills in as a guide for investigating the mind boggling trap of biodiversity that shapes the normal world. In this investigation, we dig into the domains of scientific categorization, science, and life cycles, disentangling the strings that associate every living creature.

Scientific classification:

Scientific categorization, got from the Greek words "taxis" (plan) and "nomos" (technique), is the study of arrangement. Its essential objective is to arrange living organic entities into various leveled classifications in view of their common attributes. The Linnaean framework, laid out via Carl Linnaeus in the eighteenth hundred years, shapes the groundwork of present day scientific classification. It characterizes living beings into a various leveled structure going from general classifications like spaces and realms to additional particular ones like phyla, classes, orders, families, genera, and species.

The arrangement framework mirrors the transformative connections between creatures, gathering them in view of shared family and morphological elements. Taxonomists utilize various methods, including sub-atomic science, life systems, and biology, to depict these connections. Propels in DNA sequencing innovation, specifically, have reformed scientific classification, considering more exact and exact arrangement in view of hereditary likenesses.

Science:

Science, the investigation of living creatures and their communications with the climate, envelops many disciplines. From the minuscule universe of cells to the glory of biological systems, science looks to unwind the secrets of life. At its center, science investigates the qualities, ways of behaving, and basic cycles that characterize living substances.

Cell science, a basic part of science, examines the design and capability of cells — the structure blocks of life. Life forms can be grouped into two principal types in view of cell structure: prokaryotes, coming up short on a film bound core, and eukaryotes, with an unmistakable core. The investigation of hereditary qualities and atomic science dives into the genetic data encoded in DNA, disentangling the systems overseeing legacy and advancement.

Physiology, one more fundamental part of science, inspects how life forms capability at the cell, organ, and foundational levels. Understanding physiological cycles gives bits of knowledge into variations, energy digestion, and the upkeep of homeostasis. Nature, then again, investigates the associations among organic entities and their surroundings, explaining the many-sided snare of connections that support life on The planet.

Life Cycle:

The existence pattern of a living being envelops the different phases of its presence, from birth or germination to propagation and possible passing. Life cycles are assorted, mirroring the versatility of creatures to various conditions and biological specialties. While there is impressive variety, life cycles by and large follow an example that incorporates development, improvement, proliferation, and, at last, the propagation of the species.

In plants, the existence cycle frequently includes shift of ages, with sporophyte and gametophyte stages. Sporophytes produce spores through meiosis, which bring about gametophytes through mitosis. Gametophytes, thus, produce gametes that breaker during treatment, restarting the cycle. This mind boggling life cycle gives potential open doors to variation to various natural circumstances.

Creatures, then again, show assorted life cycle systems. Bugs, for instance, ordinarily go through complete transformation, changing through egg, larval, pupal, and grown-up stages. Creatures of land and water, similar to frogs, go through transformation too, advancing from sea-going fledglings to earthbound grown-ups. Warm blooded creatures, including people, experience a more clear life cycle described by birth, development, generation, and maturing.

The existence patterns of numerous species are unpredictably connected with natural variables, like temperature, light, and food accessibility. These transformations add to the general endurance and regenerative progress of the organic entity, forming the variety of life on The planet.

Interconnected Strings:

The strings of scientific categorization, science, and life cycles are complicatedly woven, shaping an embroidery that catches the embodiment of natural variety. Scientific categorization gives the system to understanding the connections between organic entities, directing scholars in their investigation of the rules that oversee life. Science, thusly, disentangles the intricacies of living life forms, from the sub-atomic components inside cells to the connections among species and their surroundings. Life cycles, the cadenced dance of birth, development, generation, and demise, grandstand the versatility and flexibility of life structures across the tremendous range of biodiversity.

In addition, headways in innovation and logical approaches keep on improving comprehension we might interpret these interconnected strings. Sub-atomic procedures, for example, DNA barcoding, take into consideration more exact species recognizable proof and arrangement. Transformative science reveals insight into the verifiable cycles that have molded the variety of life north of millions of years. Protection science, a part of science with an emphasis on saving biodiversity, underscores the significance of understanding scientific classification and life cycles with regards to biological system wellbeing and manageability.

1.1 Taxonomic classification and key characteristics

Ordered characterization is a foundation of natural science, giving a precise structure to sorting out and classifying the monstrous variety of life on The planet. This grouping framework, established in the standards laid out via Carl Linnaeus in the eighteenth hundred years, empowers researchers to comprehend the connections between various life forms in light of shared attributes and developmental history. This thorough investigation will dive into the complexities of ordered grouping, revealing insight into its verifiable turn of events, procedures, and the key qualities that characterize each ordered level.

Verifiable Turn of events:

The foundations of ordered grouping follow back to old civilizations, where early endeavors were made to coordinate and arrange residing creatures in light of recognizable highlights. Notwithstanding, it was Carl Linnaeus who formalized an orderly methodology in the eighteenth hundred years, presenting a various leveled framework that organized living beings into bunches in light of shared morphological qualities. This Linnaean framework established the groundwork for current scientific categorization, which has developed throughout the hundreds of years with the joining of sub-atomic strategies, hereditary qualities, and a more profound comprehension of developmental connections.

Ordered Progressive system:

The ordered order is a layered framework that sorts out living life forms into continuously more comprehensive classes. The fundamental positions incorporate areas, realms, phyla, classes, orders, families, genera, and species. Each ordered level addresses a gathering of life forms that share specific qualities and developmental history. For instance, the animals of the world collectively envelops different phyla, every one of which contains particular classes, etc. This various leveled structure takes into consideration a methodical and coordinated portrayal of the variety of life.

Techniques for Ordered Characterization:

Scientific classification utilizes different techniques to characterize and classify organic entities. Customary scientific categorization depends on morphological qualities, like physical elements and regenerative designs, for arrangement. With the coming of atomic science and DNA sequencing advancements, sub-atomic scientific categorization has turned into a fundamental piece of arrangement endeavors. Contrasting hereditary material permits researchers with distinguish imparted family and refine characterizations to a more significant level of exactness.

Key Qualities at Various Ordered Levels:

At each ordered level, explicit qualities characterize and recognize gatherings of organic entities. For instance, in the animals of the world collectively, living beings share attributes like eukaryotic cells, multicellularity, and heterotrophy. As we drop down the progressive system, key elements become more refined and explicit. Vertebrates, for example, share normal qualities like hair, mammary organs, and warm-bloodedness inside the class Mammalia. The species level is portrayed by the capacity of people to interbreed and deliver rich posterity.

Area Archaea:

Inside the three spaces of life — Archaea, Microbes, and Eukarya — Archaea addresses a particular gathering of single-celled microorganisms. Archaea share qualities with the two microbes and eukaryotes however have novel highlights, for example, the organization of their cell walls and the presence of extremophiles equipped for making due in outrageous conditions.

Space Microscopic organisms:

Microscopic organisms comprise an immense and various gathering of single-celled microorganisms. They come up short on film bound core and are portrayed by their prokaryotic cell structure. Microbes assume essential parts in different biological cycles, including supplement cycling and advantageous associations with different creatures.

Space Eukarya:

Eukarya incorporates an expansive scope of life forms, including protists, organisms, plants, and creatures. Eukaryotic cells have a film bound core and organelles, recognizing them from prokaryotic cells. The variety inside Eukarya mirrors the development of complicated cell designs and multicellularity.

Plant Realm:

Plants, inside the Eukarya space, comprise a different gathering with key qualities, for example, photosynthesis, cellulose cell walls, and multicellularity. The plant realm incorporates a wide exhibit of living beings, from greeneries and greeneries to blooming plants, each adjusted to explicit natural specialties.

Growths Realm:

Growths, additionally part of the Eukarya space, are described by their heterotrophic method of sustenance and cell walls made out of chitin. They assume fundamental parts as decomposers, framing advantageous associations with plants, and in any event, causing sicknesses at times.

Animals of the world collectively:

The animals of the world collectively, one more part of Eukarya, is characterized by qualities like multicellularity, heterotrophy, and the shortfall of cell walls. Creatures show colossal variety, going from basic spineless creatures to complex vertebrates, each adjusted to their particular natural jobs.

Sub-atomic Scientific classification:

Sub-atomic scientific classification has changed the field by using hereditary data to lay out developmental connections. DNA barcoding, the utilization of explicit quality successions for species distinguishing proof, has turned into an incredible asset in characterizing creatures precisely. Sub-atomic procedures give experiences into the hereditary variety inside and between species, adding to a more nuanced comprehension of transformative examples.

Developmental Grouping:

Developmental characterization centers around gathering creatures in light of their transformative history and shared heritage. Phylogenetic trees portray the expanding examples of species, outlining their connections over the long haul. This approach considers hereditary, morphological, and social characteristics to develop a more exhaustive and dynamic characterization framework.

Utilizations of Scientific categorization:

Scientific categorization has expansive ramifications past the domain of organic characterization. Preservation science depends on exact scientific categorization to distinguish and safeguard jeopardized species. Agribusiness benefits from understanding plant scientific categorization to further develop crop yields and foster illness safe assortments. Also, scientific categorization helps clinical exploration by recognizing and concentrating on creatures with expected remedial properties.

Difficulties and Future Headings:

While ordered grouping has taken huge steps, challenges persevere. The disclosure of new species, particularly in neglected environments, presents hardships in keeping a forward-thinking scientific classification. Furthermore, the powerful idea of transformative connections and the continuous reconciliation of sub-atomic procedures present steady difficulties and open doors for refinement. The eventual fate of scientific classification lies in interdisciplinary coordinated effort, cutting edge innovations, and a proceeded with obligation to disentangling the intricacies of life on The planet.

1.2 Life cycle stages and developmental milestones

Life is a constant excursion set apart by particular stages, each portrayed by exceptional formative achievements. From the commencement of a creature to its inevitable decay, life cycles incorporate a progression of changes and accomplishments. This investigation will dig into the complexities of life cycle stages, looking at the achievements that characterize development and advancement across different creatures, including people, plants, and creatures. Understanding these stages and achievements not just reveals insight into the intricacy of life yet additionally fills in as an important structure for natural, mental, and humanistic examinations.

Life Cycle Stages:

Life cycles are an all inclusive idea, relevant to every single living creature. While the points of interest change between species, the crucial stages can be comprehensively sorted as birth or germination, development and advancement, proliferation, and senescence or maturing. Each stage is set apart by unmistakable physiological, conduct, and natural changes that add to the general educational experience of a living being.

Birth or Germination:

The underlying phase of a daily existence cycle includes the rise of another living being, whether through birth, incubating, or germination. This stage is basic as it sets the establishment for the whole life venture. In creatures, the birth cycle might shift from viviparous vertebrates giving live birth to oviparous birds laying eggs. In plants, germination is the groundbreaking system where a seed starts to grow and develop into another plant.

Development and Advancement:

The subsequent stage envelops the time of development and improvement. Creatures go through physiological, morphological, and conduct changes to adjust to their current circumstance. In creatures, this might include stages like outset, youth, puberty, and adulthood. In plants, it incorporates stages like seedling, vegetative development, and regenerative development. Formative achievements, like figuring out how to stroll in people or arriving at sexual development in creatures, mark the movement through this stage.

Multiplication:

Multiplication is a vital stage in the existence cycle, guaranteeing the progression of the species. Various organic entities utilize differed regenerative systems, from abiogenetic propagation in certain plants and basic creatures to sexual multiplication in additional complicated living beings. Regenerative achievements, similar to the main effective mating or the creation of seeds, portray this stage.

Senescence or Maturing:

The last stage includes senescence or maturing, a period where the creature encounters decrease in physiological capabilities. This stage can change in length and power, prompting passing. In certain species, maturing is drawn out, considering proceeded with commitment to the environment, while in others, it is generally short. Understanding the maturing system is pivotal for fields like gerontology and transformative science.

Human Existence Cycle Stages:

The human existence cycle is a mind boggling and multi-layered venture set apart by particular stages, each with its own arrangement of formative achievements.

Early stages:

Outset is the stage from birth to the initial two years of life. During this time, babies experience fast physical and tactile turn of events. Achievements incorporate coordinated abilities like creeping, standing, and strolling, as well as the improvement of language and social communication.

Youth:

Youth reaches out from the finish of early stages to pubescence. This stage includes further improvement of mental, profound, and interactive abilities. Key achievements incorporate language securing, the arrangement of social securities, and the improvement of an identity.

Youthfulness:

Youthfulness is a momentary stage among adolescence and adulthood, set apart by pubescence and the beginning of sexual development. Actual changes, mental turn of events, and the arrangement of character are key to this stage. Achievements incorporate the improvement of unique reasoning, the investigation of individual qualities, and the foundation of freedom.

Adulthood:

Adulthood is extensively separated into right on time, center, and late stages. Early adulthood (20s to 30s) includes the quest for instruction, vocation improvement, and the foundation of personal connections. Center adulthood (40s to 60s) sees an emphasis on family and vocation soundness. Late adulthood (60s and then some) includes reflection on life, retirement, and potential wellbeing challenges.

Senescence:

The last stage includes senescence, set apart by the physical and mental degradation related with maturing. Achievements in this stage incorporate retirement, potential medical problems, and the reflection on one's life process. The experience of senescence differs among people and is affected by hereditary, way of life, and ecological variables.

Vegetation Cycle Stages:

Plants go through a day to day existence cycle portrayed by rotation of ages, including both haploid and diploid stages. The vegetation cycle commonly incorporates the sporophyte and gametophyte ages.

Sporophyte Age:

The sporophyte age starts with the germination of a seed. It addresses the diploid stage where the plant produces spores through meiosis. These spores bring about the haploid gametophyte age.

Gametophyte Age:

The gametophyte age includes the creation of gametes through mitosis. In certain plants, similar to greeneries, the gametophyte is an unmistakable construction, while in others, such as blossoming plants, it is diminished and reliant upon the sporophyte. Treatment happens when gametes join to frame a zygote.

Seed Arrangement:

After treatment, the zygote forms into an incipient organism inside a seed. The seed gives assurance and sustenance to the creating incipient organism. It is frequently spread to new areas, advancing the plant's endurance.

Germination:

The existence cycle restarts with germination, where the seed goes through ecological prompts like dampness and warmth, starting the development of another sporophyte. This goes full circle, guaranteeing the plant's coherence.

Creature Life Cycle Stages:

Creature life cycles show extraordinary variety in light of species, however certain normal stages and achievements can be distinguished.

Undeveloped Turn of events:

Creature life cycles frequently start with undeveloped turn of events. This stage includes the arrangement and separation of cells, prompting the advancement of tissues, organs, and body structures. The particulars shift broadly, from inside development in warm blooded creatures to outside egg-laying in reptiles and birds.

Adolescent Stage:

The adolescent stage follows undeveloped turn of events and is described by quick development. Creatures procure the essential abilities for endurance, like hunting or rummaging, and may go through actual changes, like the advancement of grown-up fur or quills.

Adulthood:

Adulthood is set apart by sexual development and the capacity to imitate. This stage includes the quest for mates, romance ways of behaving, and the foundation of domains. Regenerative achievements, like the principal fruitful mating or the introduction of posterity, are vital to this stage.

Parental Consideration:

A few animal types show parental consideration, where grown-ups put time and assets in raising their posterity. Parental consideration can take different structures, from watching eggs to giving food and security to youthful creatures.

Senescence:

The last stage includes senescence, where maturing and a decrease in actual capabilities happen. The term of senescence fluctuates among species, for certain creatures displaying expanded life expectancies, while others have somewhat short lives.

Formative Achievements:

Formative achievements are key accomplishments or capacities came to during explicit phases of a creature's life cycle. These achievements differ broadly between species yet are significant marks of typical development and development.

In people, formative achievements are frequently ordered into spaces like engine, mental, social, and close to home.

Engine Advancement:

Engine advancement includes the movement of actual capacities, including gross and fine coordinated abilities. Achievements incorporate turning over, slithering, strolling, and the advancement of manual ability. In creatures, engine achievements might incorporate flying for birds or swimming for fish.

Mental Turn of events:

Mental improvement alludes to the development of mental cycles, for example, memory, critical thinking, and language obtaining. In people, achievements incorporate the rise of language, emblematic reasoning, and the advancement of unique thinking. In creatures, mental achievements might include critical abilities to think, apparatus use, or correspondence.

Social and Close to home Turn of events:

Social and close to home improvement incorporates the capacity to frame connections, direct feelings, and figure out expressive gestures. In people, achievements incorporate the development of connections, sympathy, and the improvement of a feeling of character. In creatures, social and close to home achievements might include the foundation of orders, mating ways of behaving, and parental consideration.

Regenerative Achievements:

Regenerative achievements are pivotal in the existence patterns of physically duplicating organic entities. In people, this incorporates the beginning of adolescence, the capacity to replicate, and the arrangement of personal connections. In creatures, regenerative achievements differ generally and may incorporate romance ways of behaving, effective mating, and the birth or bring forth of posterity.

Maturing Achievements:

Maturing achievements mark the progress into senescence. In people, this includes actual changes, for example, turning gray hair, mental changes, and potential wellbeing challenges. In creatures, maturing achievements might remember a downfall for actual capacities, changes in conduct, and a reduction in regenerative abilities.

Factors Affecting Turn of events:

Formative directions are impacted by a complicated transaction of hereditary, ecological, and experiential elements. Understanding these impacts is fundamental for appreciating the variety of life cycle ways.

Hereditary Variables:

Hereditary elements assume a principal part in molding a living being's formative way. Qualities decide the essential plan for physical and physiological highlights, impacting attributes like level, hue, and vulnerability to specific sicknesses.

Ecological Elements:

The climate where a creature develops and creates significantly affects its life cycle. Natural variables incorporate environment, accessibility of assets, and the presence of hunters or contenders. In people, natural factors additionally envelop financial circumstances, admittance to training, and medical care.

Dietary Elements:

Sufficient sustenance is essential for typical development and advancement. Dietary elements impact actual turn of events, mental capacities, and generally wellbeing. In plants, supplement accessibility in the dirt significantly influences germination, development, and conceptive achievement.

Social and Social Impacts:

Social and social elements shape the formative encounters of people and certain creature species. Social practices, cultural standards, and the presence of social encouraging groups of people can fundamentally influence mental, close to home, and social turn of events.

Experiential Learning:

Gaining from encounters is a crucial part of improvement. The two people and creatures obtain abilities, ways of behaving, and information through openness to their current circumstance. This experiential learning adds to versatile ways of behaving and the capacity to explore difficulties.

Applications and Suggestions:

Understanding life cycle stages and formative achievements has wide applications across different logical disciplines and down to earth fields.

Natural and Clinical Sciences:

In science and medication, understanding life cycle stages is principal for concentrating on physiological cycles, illness movement, and the advancement of clinical mediations. Formative achievements give benchmarks to surveying typical development and identifying irregularities.

Brain research and Social Sciences:

Formative brain research centers around the investigation of human and creature advancement, analyzing mental, close to home, and social achievements. Experiences from formative brain research illuminate instructive works on, nurturing techniques, and intercessions for people with formative difficulties.

Nature and Ecological Science:

Life cycle stages are basic in environmental examinations, adding to how we might interpret populace elements, biodiversity, and biological system working. Protection endeavors benefit from information on life cycles, as it helps with recognizing weak stages and executing viable safeguarding procedures.

Training and Nurturing:

Instructive practices are educated by a comprehension regarding formative achievements. Instructors utilize this information to fit instructive ways to deal with the requirements of understudies at various transformative phases. Additionally, nurturing systems benefit from a familiarity with age-suitable achievements and assumptions.

Farming and Cultivation:

In farming and cultivation, information on vegetation cycles is fundamental for streamlining crop yield and quality. Understanding formative achievements supports the planning of planting, reaping, and other development rehearses.

Difficulties and Future Headings:

While how we might interpret life cycle stages and formative achievements has progressed fundamentally, challenges remain. The intricacy of hereditary and natural associations, the variety of living things, and the requirement for inter-disciplinary methodologies present continuous difficulties and valuable open doors for future examination.

Hereditary and Epigenetic Intricacy:

The many-sided exchange among qualities and the climate adds layers of intricacy to how we might interpret improvement. The field of epigenetics, which investi-gates how natural variables impact quality articulation, acquaints new aspects with the investigation of life cycles.

Interdisciplinary Cooperation:

Tending to the complex parts of improvement requires joint effort across assorted logical disciplines, including science, brain research, social science, and natural science. Future examination ought to stress interdisciplinary ways to deal with gain exhaustive bits of knowledge.

Worldwide and Natural Effect:

As human exercises progressively influence worldwide biological systems, under-standing the existence patterns of different species becomes critical for alleviating ecological difficulties. Environmental change, living space misfortune, and contam-ination highlight the significance of concentrating on life cycles with regards to more extensive biological frameworks.

Mechanical Advances:

Mechanical progressions, especially in fields like genomics, imaging, and infor-mation examination, give new devices to concentrating on life cycles. Proceeded with advancement around there holds guarantee for uncovering beforehand un-available parts of improvement.

Moral Contemplations:

As how we might interpret life cycles develops, moral contemplations en-compassing hereditary control, helped multiplication, and preservation endeavors become seriously squeezing. Offsetting logical advancement with moral obligation is a critical thought for future exploration.

1.3 Reproductive behavior and strategies

Conceptive way of behaving and systems are major parts of the endurance and continuation of life on The planet. Across the immense range of living creatures, conceptive procedures have developed to expand the possibilities delivering posterity and guaranteeing the propagation of their species. This investigation will dig into the complexities of regenerative way of behaving, inspecting the assorted techniques utilized by different life forms, going from microorganisms and plants to bugs, well evolved creatures, and people. Understanding the components and elements affecting regenerative way of behaving gives significant experiences into the perplexing snare of life.

Fundamental Ideas:

Multiplication is the organic cycle by which new people of similar species are delivered, guaranteeing the continuation of the species over the long haul. Conceptive way of behaving includes the activities, communications, and techniques that creatures utilize to work with fruitful proliferation. This conduct is impacted by a blend of hereditary, natural, and environmental variables.

Abiogenetic Propagation:

Abiogenetic propagation includes the creation of posterity without the inclusion of gametes (sex cells). This strategy is normal in numerous microorganisms, plants, and certain creatures. Abiogenetic propagation takes into account quick populace development and is described by the age of hereditarily indistinguishable posterity, frequently alluded to as clones.

Sexual Multiplication:

Sexual multiplication includes the combination of gametes, normally from two distinct people, prompting the arrangement of hereditarily different posterity. This technique presents hereditary fluctuation, which can be favorable for variation to evolving conditions. Sexual multiplication is pervasive in creatures, plants, and a few growths.

Conceptive Systems:

Conceptive systems are assorted and adjusted to the environmental specialty and life history of every species. These systems can be comprehensively ordered into two fundamental sorts: r-chose and K-chose methodologies.

r-Chose Species:

r-Chose species are described by high conceptive rates, delivering countless posterity in a somewhat brief period. These species contribute insignificant parental consideration, and the endurance pace of individual posterity might be low. Models incorporate numerous bugs, little rodents, and certain marine organic entities.

K-Chose Species:

K-chose species show lower regenerative rates, putting additional time and assets in the consideration and advancement of less posterity. These species frequently have longer life expectancies and may show complex social ways of behaving. Well evolved creatures, including people, are regularly connected with K-chose conceptive systems.

Conceptive Conduct in Plants:

Plants utilize different conceptive systems, frequently impacted by ecological variables. Key parts of plant regenerative way of behaving incorporate fertilization, seed creation, and dispersal.

Fertilization:

Fertilization is a urgent move toward plant multiplication, including the exchange of dust (containing male gametes) to the shame of a blossom (containing female gametes). This can happen through wind, bugs, birds, or different specialists. Various plants have advanced explicit transformations to draw in pollinators, like beautiful blossoms, nectar, or scent.

Seed Creation and Dispersal:

After effective fertilization, seeds foster inside the ovary of a blossom. The dispersal of seeds is fundamental for colonizing new regions. Plants utilize different procedures, including wind dispersal, creature dispersal (by appending seeds to fur or quills), or water dispersal (seeds drifting on water), to guarantee the proliferation of their species.

Regenerative Conduct in Creatures:

Creature regenerative way of behaving is unimaginably assorted, reflecting transformations to various natural specialties, mating frameworks, and social designs.

Mating Frameworks:

Mating frameworks fluctuate broadly among creatures. Monogamy includes a drawn out pair connection between a male and a female. Polygamy incorporates both polygyny (one male mating with numerous females) and polyandry (one female mating with different guys). Wantonness alludes to various mating accomplices without framing long haul bonds.

Romance and Mate Determination:

Romance ways of behaving assume a critical part in mate choice. These ways of behaving can incorporate presentations, vocalizations, or actual customs that show the wellness and reasonableness of a person as a mate. Mate determination is impacted by different elements, including hereditary similarity, asset accessibility, and natural circumstances.

Parental Consideration:

Parental consideration is a critical part of conceptive conduct in numerous creatures. This care can incorporate structure homes, safeguarding eggs or posterity, giving food, and showing fundamental basic instincts. The degree of parental consideration differs generally among species, from none in some to broad consideration in others.

Conceptive Systems in Bugs:

Bugs show different conceptive procedures, going from easy to complex. A few bugs go through complete transformation, progressing through egg, larval, pupal, and grown-up stages. Others, similar to subterranean insects and honey bees, show eusocial conduct with a division of work among sterile and conceptive people.

Regenerative Procedures in Warm blooded animals:

Warm blooded creatures, including people, show a great many regenerative procedures. Notwithstanding different mating frameworks, warm blooded animals might display different regenerative ways of behaving, like the foundation of domains, romance customs, and elaborate parental consideration. A few well evolved creatures, similar to rodents, have short growth periods and produce different litters, while bigger vertebrates, similar to elephants, have longer development periods and focus intently on the consideration of a solitary posterity.

Human Regenerative Way of behaving:

Human conceptive way of behaving is intricate and impacted by social, social, and mental elements. Key angles incorporate mate determination, romance, family structures, and the impact of preventative advancements.

Mate Choice:

People take part in complex mate determination processes impacted by actual engaging quality, character attributes, financial status, and social elements. Developmental brain science recommends that specific characteristics are inclined toward because of their likely commitments to the endurance and prosperity of posterity.

Romance and Match Holding:

Romance ways of behaving in people envelop a large number of exercises, from verbal correspondence and shared exercises to gift-giving and shows of warmth. Match holding is a typical part of human regenerative way of behaving, including the development of long haul connections to helpfully raise posterity.

Family Designs:

Human social orders display assorted family structures, going from family units to more distant families and shared courses of action. These designs impact the appropriation of providing care liabilities and the socialization of posterity.

Contraception and Family Arranging:

The turn of events and broad utilization of prophylactic advances have significantly affected human regenerative way of behaving. Admittance to contraception permits people and couples more prominent command over family arranging, adding to changes in richness rates and family size.

Transformative Points of view:

Conceptive way of behaving is in many cases seen through a transformative focal point, taking into account how ways of behaving and procedures have developed to improve the regenerative outcome of people and species.

Sexual Determination:

Sexual determination, proposed by Charles Darwin, underlines the job of contest for mates and mate inclinations in deeply shaping conceptive way of behaving. This interaction can prompt the advancement of attributes that increment a singular's engaging quality to possible mates, regardless of whether those characteristics straightforwardly upgrade endurance.

Parental Venture Hypothesis:

Parental venture hypothesis, created by Robert Trivers, places that the sex that puts more in posterity (commonly females) will be more particular in mate decision, while the other sex (normally guys) will seek admittance to mates. This hypothesis makes sense of contrasts in mating methodologies and ways of behaving among guys and females.

Difficulties and Future Bearings:

The investigation of regenerative conduct faces progressing difficulties and open doors for investigation, especially with regards to human social orders, evolving conditions, and worldwide issues.

Human Populace Elements:

The fast development of the human populace presents difficulties connected with asset allotment, natural effect, and maintainability. Understanding human conceptive way of behaving is critical for tending to these difficulties and advancing mindful populace the board.

Environmental Change and Biodiversity Misfortune:

Ecological changes, including environmental change and natural surroundings misfortune, can affect conceptive ways of behaving in different species. Concentrating on these effects is fundamental for preservation endeavors and grasping the versatility of environments.

Innovative Advances:

Propels in conceptive advances, like in vitro treatment (IVF), hereditary designing, and quality altering, present moral contemplations and valuable open doors for affecting regenerative ways of behaving. The moral ramifications of these innovations need cautious assessment.

Social and Cultural Impacts:

The transaction between social, cultural, and individual variables in shaping regenerative way of behaving is complicated. Understanding how social standards and cultural designs impact family arranging, ripeness rates, and conceptive decisions is pivotal for tending to worldwide difficulties.

Orientation and Regenerative Wellbeing:

Orientation elements assume a huge part in regenerative way of behaving. Guaranteeing fair admittance to regenerative wellbeing administrations, instruction, and family arranging choices is fundamental for tending to abberations and advancing the prosperity of people and networks.

Chapter 2

Distribution, Habitat, And Ecology

Dissemination alludes to the geological region or reach where a specific animal varieties, populace, or local area of creatures is found. The conveyance of living life forms is impacted by a heap of variables, including natural circumstances, environmental cooperations, and verifiable cycles. Understanding conveyance designs is critical for scientists, protectionists, and policymakers, as it gives experiences into the environmental prerequisites and reactions of living beings to their environmental elements.

Factors Affecting Circulation:

The dispersion of living beings is formed by both abiotic and biotic elements. Abiotic factors incorporate environment, geology, soil creation, and water accessibility. Biotic variables include communications with other living creatures, like contest, predation, and mutualism. Moreover, verifiable variables, as transformative cycles and topographical occasions, assume a part in deciding the dissemination of species over the long run.

Worldwide and Nearby Scales:

Appropriation examples can be inspected at various scales, from worldwide disseminations of whole species to nearby conveyances inside unambiguous natural surroundings. At a worldwide scale, factors like environment and mainland float impact the wide conveyance of species, while at a nearby scale, factors, for example, microclimates, soil types, and neighborhood species collaborations become more persuasive.

Endemism and Cosmopolitanism:

Endemism alludes to the limitation of an animal categories to a particular geographic region, frequently because of novel biological circumstances. Conversely, cosmopolitan species have a broad dispersion across various locales. Understanding the appropriation of endemic species is indispensable for protection endeavors, as these species are many times more defenseless against territory misfortune and ecological changes.

Human Impact on Dissemination:

Human exercises, including territory obliteration, contamination, and environmental change, altogether influence the dispersion of numerous species. The presentation of non-local species and modification of regular living spaces add to changes in dissemination designs, frequently prompting environmental uneven characters and biodiversity misfortune.

Natural surroundings:

Natural surroundings alludes to the particular climate where a life form or local area of creatures resides and flourishes. Living spaces give the vital assets and conditions for endurance, including food, water, cover, and appropriate natural variables. The idea of territory is fundamental to natural examinations as it impacts the dispersion and wealth of species.

Kinds of Environments:

Natural surroundings arrive in a wide cluster of structures, each portrayed by unambiguous abiotic and biotic circumstances. Earthbound natural surroundings incorporate woodlands, prairies, deserts, and wetlands, while amphibian territories include freshwater biological systems like streams and lakes, as well as marine conditions like seas and coral reefs.

Microhabitats:

Inside bigger natural surroundings, organic entities frequently possess explicit microhabitats that meet their particular requirements. For instance, in a woods territory, microhabitats can incorporate the backwoods floor, the covering, and tree rind, each giving remarkable circumstances to different creatures.

Specialty and Environment Determination:

The natural specialty of an animal groups characterizes its job and necessities in an environment. Environment determination includes the interaction by which creatures pick explicit territories that best suit their biological requirements. This interaction is impacted by elements like asset accessibility, contest, and predation risk.

Environment Discontinuity:

Human exercises, like urbanization and farming, can prompt environment discontinuity, where enormous, nonstop territories are broken into more modest, segregated patches. This can fundamentally affect biodiversity, as it influences the capacity of species to move, track down mates, and access assets.

Biology:

Biology is the logical investigation of the connections among creatures and their current circumstance. It envelops an expansive scope of subjects, including the dispersion and overflow of organic entities, the progression of energy and supplements through environments, and the cooperations between various species.

Levels of Environmental Association:

Environment works at different degrees of association, from individual life forms to populaces, networks, biological systems, and the biosphere. Understanding how cooperations at each level impact the general working of environments is crucial to natural examination.

Environment Construction and Capability:

Biological systems are made out of biotic parts (living creatures) and abiotic parts (non-living elements). The design of a biological system alludes to the arrangement and association of its parts, while capability depicts the cycles and connections that support life inside the environment. Key environment processes incorporate energy stream and supplement cycling.

Biotic Cooperations:

Biotic cooperations in biological systems incorporate different types of beneficial interaction, rivalry, predation, and mutualism. These cooperations shape populace elements, impact species conveyance, and add to the general solidness and versatility of biological systems.

Biogeochemical Cycles:

Biogeochemical cycles, like the carbon, nitrogen, and phosphorus cycles, depict the development of fundamental components through living organic entities, the climate, soil, and water. These cycles are basic for keeping up with the accessibility of supplements fundamental forever.

Progression and Aggravation:

Biological progression alludes to the course of progress in the sythesis of species after some time in a specific natural surroundings. Aggravations, like rapidly spreading fires or human exercises, can disturb biological systems and start progression. Understanding these cycles is fundamental for anticipating biological system reactions to natural changes.

Protection Biology:

Protection biology centers around understanding and saving biodiversity. This includes concentrating on the effects of human exercises on environments, recognizing jeopardized species, and creating techniques for territory rebuilding and protection.

Applications and Significance:

Environment has expansive ramifications and applications in different fields, adding to how we might interpret regular frameworks and illuminating procedures for maintainable asset the executives and preservation.

Maintainable Asset The executives:

Biological standards guide the practical administration of normal assets, including fisheries, ranger service, and horticulture. By understanding the elements of biological systems, researchers and policymakers can foster practices that limit natural effect and guarantee the drawn out accessibility of assets.

Environmental Change and Transformation:

Nature assumes a significant part in concentrating on the effects of environmental change on biological systems and distinguishing techniques for transformation and relief. Understanding how species and biological systems answer changing natural circumstances is fundamental for anticipating future environmental elements.

Reclamation Biology:

Rebuilding environment centers around the recovery of corrupted biological systems. By applying environmental standards, researchers can foster methodologies to reestablish territories, once again introduce local species, and upgrade biodiversity in regions affected by human exercises.

Human Wellbeing and Biology:

The soundness of environments straightforwardly impacts human prosperity. Biological investigations assist with distinguishing joins between natural elements, like air and water quality, and human wellbeing results. This information is basic for general wellbeing and ecological administration.

Difficulties and Future Headings:

Nature faces continuous difficulties and open doors as scientists try to resolve complex ecological issues, including territory misfortune, environmental change, and biodiversity decline.

Worldwide Change and Biodiversity Misfortune:

Human-instigated changes, including natural surroundings obliteration, contamination, and environmental change, present critical dangers to biodiversity. Understanding the instruments driving these progressions is fundamental for creating powerful protection systems.

Arising Irresistible Infections:

Biological elements assume a part in the development and spread of irresistible illnesses. Concentrating on the cooperations between microorganisms, has, and the climate is significant for anticipating and forestalling illness flare-ups.

Metropolitan Nature:

As urbanization keeps, concentrating on metropolitan biological systems turns out to be progressively significant. Metropolitan nature investigates what urban areas mean for biodiversity, air and water quality, and the prosperity of human populaces. Maintainable metropolitan arranging depends on biological standards to make strong and sound urban communities.

Innovative Advances:

Propels in innovation, including remote detecting, atomic science, and computational displaying, give new apparatuses to biological examination. These advancements empower scientists to gather and break down enormous datasets, improving comprehension we might interpret complex environmental cycles.

Interdisciplinary Coordinated effort:

Tending to natural difficulties requires interdisciplinary cooperation. Biologists work close by specialists in fields like financial aspects, social science, and designing to foster comprehensive arrangements that offset human requirements with natural maintainability.

2.1 Geographic range and habitats in Atlantic Waters

The Atlantic Sea, one of the world's significant seas, is a tremendous and dynamic waterway that impacts the environment, biodiversity, and human exercises on a worldwide scale. Understanding the geographic reach and territories inside Atlantic waters is fundamental for grasping the complex biological frameworks, species dispersions, and the interconnectedness of marine life. This investigation will dig into the different and extraordinary biological systems that characterize the Atlantic, including its breadths from the Icy to the Antarctic.

Geographic Reach:

The Atlantic Sea traverses an immense region, extending from the Icy Sea in the north toward the Southern Sea in the south. It is lined by the Americas toward the west and Europe and Africa toward the east. The North Atlantic and South Atlantic are many times recognized in light of their latitudinal areas, each displaying particular climatic examples, sea flows, and biological systems.

Cold and Subarctic Districts:

In the northernmost spans, the Atlantic Sea stretches out into the Cold area. Here, the Atlantic impacts the environment and ocean ice elements, affecting the fragile equilibrium of the Cold biological system. Species like polar bears, seals, and different seabirds are adjusted to the exceptional states of the Cold waters.

Mild Zones:

The mild zones of the North Atlantic are portrayed by a blend of cold and warm flows. These zones support different marine life, including different fish species, marine warm blooded creatures, and seabirds. The Bay Stream, a strong warm current, impacts the environment and biodiversity along the eastern shore of North America and Western Europe.

Central and Tropical Areas:

As the Atlantic methodologies the equator, it enters tropical and subtropical areas. Coral reefs, described by high biodiversity, flourish in the warm waters of the Caribbean and portions of the West African coast. These districts are home to a wealth of marine species, including bright reef fish, coral species, and marine spineless creatures.

South Atlantic:

The South Atlantic, stretching out to the Antarctic Circumpolar Current, displays special elements contrasted with its northern partner. Coldwater species, like penguins and seals, are adjusted to the freezing states of the Southern Sea. Antarctic waters are home to krill, a basic part of the Southern Sea food web.

Living spaces in Atlantic Waters:

The Atlantic Sea incorporates a wide assortment of territories, going from shallow waterfront regions to remote ocean conditions. Every natural surroundings upholds an unmistakable exhibit of animal groups and biological cycles, adding to the general wellbeing and biodiversity of the Atlantic.

Waterfront and Intertidal Zones:

Waterfront and intertidal zones along the Atlantic coasts are dynamic natural surroundings impacted by flowing vacillations. These regions are described by rough shores, sandy sea shores, and estuaries. Mangrove backwoods, tracked down in tropical and subtropical beach front regions, give fundamental nurseries to fish and go about as defensive cushions against storm floods.

Coral Reefs:

Coral reefs are noticeable in tropical Atlantic waters, supporting lively and different biological systems. The Caribbean, specifically, is known for coral reefs give environment to a heap of fish animal groups, spineless creatures, and marine plants. Coral reefs are exceptionally delicate to ecological changes, making them helpless against environmental change and human effects.

Untamed Sea and Pelagic Zone:

The tremendous untamed sea, known as the pelagic zone, covers most of the Atlantic. Inside this environment, marine life goes from minuscule tiny fish to enormous pelagic species like sharks, fishes, and whales. Sea flows and upwelling zones assume a critical part in supplement cycling and supporting the efficiency of the pelagic environment.

Remote ocean Conditions:

The Atlantic Sea contains broad remote ocean conditions, including deep fields, seamounts, and aqueous vent frameworks. Remote ocean environments are portrayed by outrageous strain, cold temperatures, and restricted light. Adjusted species, like remote ocean fish and spineless creatures, flourish in these difficult circumstances.

Mid-Atlantic Edge:

The Mid-Atlantic Edge, a conspicuous submerged mountain range running down the focal point of the Atlantic Sea, fills in as a special living space. Aqueous vents along the edge support environments that depend on chemosynthesis instead of daylight for energy. These vent networks are home to specific living beings adjusted to the outrageous states of high strain and temperature.

Seagrass Glades and Algal Beds:

Seagrass knolls and algal beds are fundamental waterfront natural surroundings tracked down in shallow Atlantic waters. These natural surroundings give basic rearing and taking care of justification for different marine species, including fish and shellfish. Seagrasses add to carbon sequestration and balance out waterfront dregs.

Biological system Administrations and Human Effect:

The Atlantic Sea assumes an imperative part in giving environment benefits that support life and backing human prosperity. Fisheries, the travel industry, environment guideline, and social importance are among the many administrations gotten from Atlantic biological systems.

Fisheries:

The Atlantic is a huge wellspring of fisheries assets, supporting the livelihoods of seaside networks and adding to worldwide fish utilization. Supportable fisheries the executives is vital to forestall overfishing and keep up with the soundness of marine populaces.

The travel industry:

Beach front region of the Atlantic, particularly in tropical locales, draw in large number of sightseers every year. Coral reefs, sandy sea shores, and marine natural life add to the financial worth of the travel industry. Manageable the travel industry rehearses are fundamental to limit adverse consequences on delicate marine environments.

Environment Guideline:

The Atlantic Sea assumes a basic part in managing worldwide environment designs. Sea ebbs and flows, for example, the Inlet Stream, impact local environments along the eastern shores of North America and Western Europe. The retention of carbon dioxide by Atlantic waters adds to environment guideline by alleviating ozone depleting substance levels.

Biodiversity Preservation:

The different living spaces inside Atlantic waters are home to a huge swath of marine species. Biodiversity preservation endeavors plan to safeguard weak species, save one of a kind living spaces, and keep up with the general flexibility of marine biological systems notwithstanding human-incited and ecological difficulties.

Anthropogenic Dangers:

Human exercises present critical dangers to Atlantic biological systems. Overfishing, natural surroundings obliteration, contamination, and environmental change endanger the soundness of marine conditions. Moderating these dangers requires global collaboration, practical asset the board, and preservation systems that focus on environment wellbeing.

Protection and The executives:

Monitoring the wellbeing and biodiversity of Atlantic waters requires facilitated protection and the board endeavors. Peaceful accords, marine safeguarded regions, and reasonable practices assume a vital part in protecting the eventual fate of Atlantic environments.

Marine Safeguarded Regions (MPAs):

Laying out marine safeguarded regions is a key preservation system to save basic territories and biodiversity. MPAs can add to the recuperation of overexploited fish stocks, safeguard weak species, and keep up with the flexibility of biological systems.

Global Participation:

The interconnected idea of the Atlantic Sea requires global cooperation for successful preservation and the executives. Provincial fisheries the executives associations, natural arrangements, and drives, for example, the Unified Countries Ten years of Sea Science for Feasible Improvement mean to address transboundary challenges.

Reasonable Fisheries The executives:

Executing supportable fisheries the board rehearses is fundamental to forestall overfishing and keep up with the wellbeing of fish populaces. Science-based approaches, including stock evaluations and environment based administration, add to the feasible utilization of marine assets.

Environmental Change Variation:

Environmental change presents huge difficulties to Atlantic biological systems, including increasing ocean temperatures, sea fermentation, and changing precipitation designs. Transformation techniques include observing and relieving the effects of environmental change on marine life and biological systems.

Local area Commitment and Instruction:

Including nearby networks in protection endeavors and advancing natural schooling are significant parts of fruitful marine preservation. Building mindfulness about the significance of Atlantic biological systems cultivates a feeling of stewardship and energizes manageable practices.

2.2 Environmental requirements and factors influencing distribution

Natural prerequisites and variables affecting circulation are basic ideas in environment, forming the spatial conveyance of species and deciding their progress in various territories. The cooperation among life forms and their current circumstance is many-sided, with different biotic and abiotic factors assuming crucial parts. This investigation digs into the ecological prerequisites of living life forms and the large number of variables that impact their conveyance across earthly, amphibian, and elevated environments.

Ecological Prerequisites:

Creatures show explicit ecological necessities that direct their endurance, development, and generation. These prerequisites can be extensively ordered into abiotic factors, like environment, soil, and water, and biotic elements, incorporating connections with different species and accessibility of assets.

Environment:

Environment is an essential ecological variable impacting the dispersion of life forms. Temperature, precipitation, dampness, and daylight assume critical parts in deciding if a specific locale is reasonable for a given animal types. Living beings have developed to flourish in unambiguous climatic circumstances, prompting the arrangement of unmistakable biomes, like deserts, rainforests, and tundras.

Soil Creation:

Soil attributes, including surface, pH, supplement content, and waste, significantly influence the conveyance of plant species. Various plants have explicit soil prerequisites, prompting the development of extraordinary plant networks in different soil types, for example, sandy soils, dirt soils, and loamy soils.

Water Accessibility:

Water is an essential asset forever, and its accessibility unequivocally impacts the dissemination of creatures. Oceanic creatures are straightforwardly reliant upon water, while earthbound living beings frequently have explicit variations to adapt to changing water accessibility. Dry season safe plants, for example, have developed systems to moderate water in bone-dry conditions.

Geology:

The actual highlights of the scene, including rise, incline, and angle, add to the ecological prerequisites of living beings. Elevated species, for instance, are adjusted to the difficulties of high-height conditions, while species in swamp regions might have various transformations fit to their particular geographical setting.

Biotic Collaborations:

Collaborations with other living creatures, both of the equivalent and various species, impact natural necessities. Predation, rivalry for assets, mutualistic connections, and beneficial interaction shape the circulation and overflow of species. For example, the presence of a particular plant might draw in specific pollinators, influencing the conveyance of both plant and pollinator species.

Factors Impacting Conveyance:

The conveyance of creatures is impacted by a mind boggling exchange of variables, and understanding these elements is fundamental for anticipating how species answer ecological changes. These variables can be classified into dispersal systems, authentic elements, natural collaborations, and anthropogenic impacts.

Dispersal Systems:

Dispersal systems assume a critical part in deciding how species colonize new regions. A few animal types have powerful dispersal systems, for example, wind-scattered seeds, creature dispersal through fur or quills, or sea-going organic entities conveyed by sea flows. Dispersal capacity can impact the rate at which species can colonize or recolonize living spaces.

Authentic Variables:

Authentic occasions, including glaciations, land developments, and transformative cycles, shape the circulation of species throughout geographical time scales. For instance, the development of mainlands and the arrangement of land spans have impacted the appropriation of both earthbound and amphibian creatures.

Biological Connections:

Communications between species, like rivalry, predation, and mutualism, assume a urgent part in deciding the dissemination of creatures. Serious rejection might limit the conveyance of firmly related species with comparative environmental prerequisites, while mutualistic communications can upgrade the endurance and development of the two species included.

Anthropogenic Impacts:

Human exercises altogether influence the dissemination of species. Territory obliteration, contamination, environmental change, and the presentation of non-local species can modify biological systems, disturb regular dissemination examples, and lead to the downfall or termination of local species. Understanding and alleviating these anthropogenic impacts are basic for protection endeavors.

Environmental Change:

Environmental change is a contemporary component applying significant consequences for the dissemination of species. Changes in temperature, precipitation examples, and ocean levels adjust the natural surroundings accessible to organic entities. A few animal varieties might adjust to these changes, while others might confront difficulties in finding reasonable natural surroundings, prompting shifts in dissemination ranges.

Earthly Conditions:

Earthly conditions, enveloping various biological systems from deserts to woodlands, display assorted ecological prerequisites and variables impacting dispersion.

Deserts:

Deserts, described by dry circumstances and restricted vegetation, have living beings adjusted to monitor water and endure high temperatures. Xerophytic plants and creatures with specific variations, for example, nighttime movement to stay away from daytime heat, flourish in desert conditions.

Prairies:

Meadows, including savannas and grasslands, are overwhelmed by herbaceous vegetation. Slow eaters and programs exist together with grasses, and fire assumes a part in keeping up with these environments. The conveyance of meadow species is impacted by elements like fire recurrence and herbivore populaces.

Woods:

Woods, going from tropical rainforests to calm and boreal timberlands, grandstand particular ecological prerequisites. The appropriation of tree species is affected by variables like temperature, precipitation, soil piece, and the presence of explicit mycorrhizal affiliations.

Rugged Districts:

Rocky areas, with fluctuating heights and geographies, have particular verdure adjusted to elevation related difficulties. Treeline ecotones, for instance, mark the progress from forested regions to snow capped conditions, impacting the appropriation of plant species.

Sea-going Conditions:

Sea-going conditions, including seas, streams, lakes, and wetlands, have their own arrangement of natural prerequisites and elements affecting the dispersion of oceanic creatures.

Marine Conditions:

Marine conditions display many environments, from coral reefs to remote ocean channels. Saltiness, temperature, sea flows, and supplement accessibility impact the dispersion of marine species. Coral reefs, for example, require explicit temperature ranges for the development of harmonious green growth critical to their wellbeing.

Freshwater Environments:

Freshwater biological systems, including streams, lakes, and wetlands, have particular natural prerequisites. Water stream, supplement levels, and temperature impact the circulation of amphibian plants, fish, and spineless creatures. The presence of explicit substrates and vegetation might impact the environment inclinations of amphibian species.

Estuaries:

Estuaries, where freshwater meets saltwater, establish remarkable conditions with changing saltiness angles. Organic entities adjusted to harsh water conditions, like specific fish and spineless creatures, occupy estuarine environments. Flowing impacts and supplement accessibility assume critical parts in estuarine natural surroundings.

Polar Locales:

Polar locales, including the Icy and Antarctic, present outrageous natural circumstances. Ocean ice elements, low temperatures, and restricted daylight shape the dispersion of polar species. Ice-adjusted organic entities, like polar bears and penguins, have advanced to flourish in these unforgiving conditions.

Ethereal Conditions:

Ethereal conditions, including the air and the surfaces of plants and designs, likewise have explicit natural necessities affecting the dispersion of airborne organic entities.

Air:

The actual air is an environment for airborne organic entities, including microbes, parasites, and different minute particles. Wind examples, stickiness, and temperature impact the dispersal and circulation of these airborne substances. A few microscopic organisms and growths assume parts in cloud development and precipitation.

Plants and Designs:

Elevated surfaces of plants and designs, for example, tree limbs and structures, give territories to organic entities like epiphytes, lichens, and certain bugs. Microclimatic conditions, substrate accessibility, and the presence of host life forms add to the dissemination of species in these flying natural surroundings.

Difficulties and Preservation Suggestions:

Understanding the natural necessities and variables affecting appropriation is significant for tending to preservation challenges and executing powerful administration procedures.

Living space Misfortune and Discontinuity:

Living space misfortune and discontinuity, frequently determined by human exercises like deforestation and urbanization, disturb the dispersion of species. Protection endeavors center around safeguarding and reestablishing natural surroundings to keep up with suitable populaces and backing environment wellbeing.

Obtrusive Species:

The presentation of non-local species can inconveniently affect local environments. Obtrusive species may outcompete or go after local species, prompting shifts in conveyance designs. Protection measures incorporate checking and controlling the spread of obtrusive species.

Environmental Change Effects:

Environmental change presents critical difficulties to species conveyance. Protection methodologies include surveying the weakness of species to environmental change, recognizing potential refugia, and executing measures to upgrade species' versatility to changing ecological circumstances.

Overexploitation and Contamination:

Overexploitation of regular assets and contamination, including air and water contamination, can significantly affect the circulation of species. Preservation endeavors center around supportable asset the executives, lessening contamination, and advancing capable practices.

Protection Arranging:

Compelling preservation arranging includes distinguishing basic living spaces, surveying the necessities of jeopardized or compromised species, and carrying out measures to safeguard biodiversity. Preservation saves, safeguarded regions, and passages are indispensable parts of protection systems to keep up with and improve species dissemination.

2.3 Feeding habits, dietary preferences, and ecological interactions

Taking care of propensities, dietary inclinations, and biological associations are basic parts of the mind boggling trap of life that characterizes environments. Understanding how organic entities acquire and eat their food, the sorts of diets they like, and their associations with different species is major to unwinding the elements of natural networks. This investigation digs into the assorted taking care of systems utilized by organic entities across various taxa, featuring the environmental meaning of these ways of behaving and their job in molding the equilibrium of nature.

Taking care of Propensities:

Taking care of propensities envelop the scope of ways of behaving and techniques life forms utilize to get and devour food. These propensities are different and are molded by developmental variations, natural specialties, and the accessibility of assets.

Herbivores:

Herbivores are essential shoppers that principally feed on plant matter. They have specific variations, like level grating teeth and complex stomach related frameworks, to remove supplements from cellulose-rich plant material. Models incorporate brushing well evolved creatures like deer, elephants, and herbivorous bugs like caterpillars.

Carnivores:

Carnivores are customers that principally feed on creature tissues. They show different hunting methodologies, from pursuit hunters to snare hunters. Rapacious transformations incorporate sharp teeth, strong jaws, and concentrated stomach related frameworks. Models range from enormous hunters like lions and wolves to more modest carnivores like bugs and falcons.

Omnivores:

Omnivores have an adaptable eating routine, benefiting from both plant and creature matter. Their flexibility permits them to take advantage of an assortment of food sources, making them adaptable shoppers. People, bears, and certain bird species are instances of omnivores that can eat many food sources in light of accessibility and healthful necessities.

Detritivores:

Detritivores feed on dead natural matter, assuming a urgent part in deterioration and supplement cycling. Organic entities like foragers, manure insects, and decomposer growths separate natural material into less difficult mixtures, working with the arrival of supplements to the environment.

Channel Feeders:

Channel feeders separate food particles from water by sifting them through specific designs. This taking care of methodology is normal among oceanic life forms, including bivalves like mollusks, whales, and certain types of fish. Channel taking care of is an effective method for catching little particles like microscopic fish.

Parasites:

Parasites get supplements by living in or on a host life form. This taking care of technique frequently includes a nearby relationship with the host, and parasites can have complex life cycles. Models incorporate parasitic worms, ticks, and a few types of organisms that contaminate plants.

Dietary Inclinations:

Dietary inclinations allude to the particular sorts of food that creatures favor in light of their healthful necessities, stomach related capacities, and environmental jobs inside biological systems.

Experts versus Generalists:

A few animal varieties are dietary trained professionals, depending on a tight scope of food sources. For instance, the koala is specific to benefit from eucalyptus leaves. Conversely, generalists have a more extensive eating routine, permitting them to adjust to an assortment of food sources. Raccoons and certain bird species are instances of dietary generalists.

Granivores and Frugivores:

Granivores represent considerable authority in consuming seeds, while frugivores principally eat natural products. Birds like finches are granivores, depending on seeds as an essential food source. Frugivores, like birds, bats, and primates, assume a urgent part in seed dispersal and the recovery of plant populaces.

Nectivores:

Nectivores feed on nectar, frequently utilizing specific variations like long proboscises or brushes to remove the sweet fluid from blossoms. Hummingbirds, honey bees, and certain bat species are instances of nectivores that add to fertilization while acquiring energy from flower nectar.

Folivores:

Folivores spend significant time in consuming leaves. Their stomach related frameworks are adjusted to separate the complicated plant cell walls and concentrate supplements from foliage. Models incorporate herbivorous bugs like caterpillars and enormous vertebrates like giraffes.

Insectivores:

Insectivores fundamentally feed on bugs and different spineless creatures. They utilize different hunting techniques, like dynamic pursuit, trap, or rummaging. Insectivorous birds, vertebrates, and reptiles add to bother control and assist with managing bug populaces.

Scroungers:

Scroungers feed on carcass or rotting natural matter. They assume an indispensable natural part by reusing supplements from dead life forms once more into the environment. Models incorporate vultures, hyenas, and particular kinds of creepy crawlies.

Biological Connections:

Biological connections include the connections between organic entities inside environments, affecting populace elements, local area structure, and the general working of natural frameworks.

Predation:

Predation includes one creature (hunter) catching and consuming another life form (prey). Predation impacts the dispersion and wealth of species in biological systems, prompting variations like disguise, cautioning shading, and protective ways of behaving in prey species.

Rivalry:

Contest happens when creatures strive for similar restricted assets, like food, water, or region. Interspecific rivalry includes contest between various species, while intraspecific rivalry happens inside similar species. Contest can drive normal determination, prompting variations that decrease rivalry or work with asset dividing.

Mutualism:

Mutualistic cooperations benefit both associating species. Models incorporate fertilization, where blooming plants and pollinators like honey bees benefit one another, and cooperative connections, for example, the mutualistic relationship among clownfish and ocean anemones.

Commensalism:

Commensalism is a relationship where one life form benefits, and the other is neither benefited nor hurt. For instance, barnacles join themselves to whales, involving the whale as a substrate for connection without hurting the host.

Parasitism:

Parasitism includes one creature (parasite) benefiting to the detriment of another life form (have). Parasites can altogether affect have populaces and may impact ways of behaving or physiological cycles to upgrade their endurance and generation.

Amensalism:

Amensalism is a relationship where one living being is adversely impacted, while the other is unaffected. For example, allelopathic plants discharge synthetic substances that repress the development of adjoining plants with no advantage to themselves.

Cornerstone Species:

Certain species, known as cornerstone species, assume excessively huge parts in keeping up with the construction and working of environments. The expulsion of a cornerstone animal types can have flowing impacts all through the whole biological system.

Beavers as Biological system Designers:

Beavers, for instance, are viewed as environment engineers. Their dam-building exercises make wetlands, changing the scene and affecting the dispersion of various plant and creature species. Wetlands give living space to various life forms and add to water filtration.

Ocean Otters in Kelp Woods:

Ocean otters are cornerstone species in kelp woods biological systems. By going after ocean imps, ocean otters control imp populaces, forestalling overgrazing on kelp. This, thus, permits the kelp to flourish, giving territory to various marine species.

Wolves in Yellowstone:

Wolves, once again introduced to Yellowstone Public Park, have significantly affected the dissemination of herbivores. By controlling elk populaces, wolves in a roundabout way impact vegetation, bird populaces, and, surprisingly, the way of behaving of waterways. This shows the broad effects of cornerstone species on environment elements.

Human Effect on Taking care of Propensities and Natural Associations:

Human exercises have critical ramifications for taking care of propensities, dietary inclinations, and natural associations. Anthropogenic impacts can upset regular natural cycles and adjust the conveyance and conduct of species.

Environment Obliteration and Discontinuity:

Environment obliteration and discontinuity, frequently determined by urbanization and rural development, upset taking care of natural surroundings and biological collaborations. Species subject to explicit natural surroundings might confront difficulties in finding appropriate food sources and reproducing locales.

Overharvesting and Overfishing:

Overharvesting of normal assets, including overfishing, can prompt decreases in populaces and upset food networks. Unreasonable reaping practices can influence the conveyance of species, especially those focused on for business purposes.

Presentation of Obtrusive Species:

The presentation of non-local species can have flowing impacts on taking care of propensities and environmental communications. Obtrusive species may outcompete local species for assets, prompting shifts in local area design and adjusting the elements of food networks.

Environmental Change:

Environmental change impacts the dispersion of species by modifying temperature and precipitation designs. Changes in environment can influence the accessibility of food sources, prompting shifts in taking care of propensities and possibly affecting the outcome of specific species.

Contamination:

Contamination, including air, water, and soil contamination, can negatively affect taking care of environments and dietary inclinations. Pollutants can amass in food sources, prompting bioaccumulation and biomagnification in food networks.

Abuse of Pesticides and Herbicides:

The abuse of pesticides and herbicides in farming can affect the overflow and variety of species. Non-target organic entities might be impacted, upsetting biological communications and prompting unseen side-effects in environments.

Protection and The board Systems:

Protection and the board systems are significant for alleviating the effects of human exercises on taking care of propensities, dietary inclinations, and natural cooperations. These systems mean to safeguard biodiversity, reestablish natural surroundings, and advance feasible practices.

Safeguarded Regions and Stores:

Laying out safeguarded regions and stores helps protect normal natural surroundings and give places of refuge to species to take care of, breed, and cooperate.

Preservation regions add to keeping up with biodiversity and safeguarding cornerstone species basic for environment wellbeing.

Reasonable Asset The executives:

Executing feasible asset the board rehearses is fundamental for guaranteeing the accessibility of food sources and limiting overharvesting. Feasible fishing rehearses, dependable ranger service, and preservation arranged farming add to keeping up with biological equilibrium.

Natural surroundings Reclamation:

Territory reclamation drives center around reestablishing corrupted environments to their regular states. Reestablished environments give fundamental assets to species, including food and rearing locales, and add to the recuperation of undermined populaces.

Obtrusive Species The executives:

Overseeing intrusive species is basic for protecting regular environmental associations. Control measures, for example, the expulsion of intrusive plants or the presentation of normal hunters, assist with moderating the effects of obtrusive species on local biological systems.

Environmental Change Moderation and Transformation:

Tending to environmental change through moderation methodologies, like lessening ozone harming substance emanations, is urgent for limiting its effect on taking care of natural surroundings and biological communications. Variation methodologies include helping species in acclimating to changing natural circumstances.

Local area Commitment and Instruction:

Including nearby networks in preservation endeavors and advancing ecological training are fundamental parts of fruitful protection techniques. Building mindfulness about the significance of protecting normal environments and advancing manageable practices cultivates a feeling of stewardship.

Chapter 3

Fisheries And Commercial Importance

Fisheries assume a basic part in giving food, livelihoods, and monetary open doors around the world. As a vital part of worldwide food frameworks, fisheries contribute essentially to sustenance, exchange, and business. This investigation dives into the complex universe of fisheries, analyzing their biological, financial, and social aspects, while likewise considering the difficulties and feasible practices important to guarantee the proceeded with business significance of this imperative asset.

Environmental Elements of Fisheries:

Biodiversity and Biological system Wellbeing:

Fisheries are necessary to marine and freshwater biological systems, interfacing with different species and adding to the many-sided equilibrium of biodiversity. Reasonable fisheries the board is fundamental for keeping up with biological system wellbeing, forestalling overexploitation, and safeguarding the perplexing snare of life inside oceanic conditions.

Life Accounts and Conceptive Systems:

Understanding the existence accounts and conceptive systems of fish species is essential for practical fisheries the board. Various species display shifted conceptive ways of behaving, development rates, and relocation designs. Successful administration systems consider these variables to guarantee the versatility of fish populaces.

Effect of Environmental Change:

Environmental change presents critical difficulties to fisheries, influencing sea temperatures, flows, and the dissemination of marine species. Changes in ocean levels and sea fermentation further compound the difficulties for both wild catch fisheries and hydroponics. Versatile administration is urgent to address the effects of environmental change on fisheries.

Sorts of Fisheries:

Distinctive Fisheries:

High quality fisheries include limited scope, frequently conventional, fishing rehearses led by nearby networks. These fisheries are described by the utilization of little boats and customary stuff. Distinctive fishers assume a fundamental part in seaside networks, adding to food security and neighborhood economies.

Modern Fisheries:

Modern or business fisheries utilize bigger vessels and cutting edge innovations to get fish for a bigger scope. These activities are frequently determined by market requests and contribute essentially to worldwide fish creation. The modern fishing area faces difficulties connected with overcapacity, bycatch, and ecological effect.

Hydroponics:

Hydroponics, or fish cultivating, has turned into an inexorably significant part of worldwide fisheries. It includes the development of sea-going organic entities in controlled conditions, going from freshwater lakes to seaward marine offices. Hydroponics adds to satisfying the developing need for fish however requires cautious administration to address ecological worries.

Sporting Fisheries:

Sporting fisheries include non-business fishing exercises sought after for game or recreation. Fishermen focus on different fish species in freshwater and marine conditions. Economical administration works on, including catch-and-delivery projects and size limits, are fundamental to keep up with the soundness of sporting fish stocks.

Business Significance and Financial Effect:

Worldwide Exchange and Market Elements:

Fisheries financially affect worldwide exchange. Fish is a profoundly exchanged ware, with nations trading and bringing in fish items to satisfy customer need. The elements of the fish market are affected by variables like customer inclinations, administrative structures, and peaceful accords.

Business and Jobs:

Fisheries give business and jobs to a great many individuals around the world. From high quality fishers in waterfront towns to laborers in handling plants and the hydroponics business, fisheries assume a focal part in supporting networks. Business open doors range from collecting to handling, advertising, and circulation.

Food Security and Sustenance:

Fish and fish are significant wellsprings of protein, fundamental supplements, and omega-3 unsaturated fats for billions of individuals all around the world. Fisheries contribute fundamentally to food security, especially in beach front districts where fish are much of the time an essential protein source. Supportable fisheries the executives is basic to guarantee proceeded with admittance to nutritious fish.

Social Significance:

Fisheries have social importance in numerous networks, forming customs, ceremonies, and personalities. Fishing rehearses are in many cases well established in the social legacy of beach front and fishing networks. Safeguarding these social viewpoints is a fundamental thought in maintainable fisheries the executives.

Challenges in Fisheries The executives:

Overfishing and Exhausting Stocks:

Overfishing happens when the pace of fishing surpasses the normal proliferation limit of fish stocks. This can prompt the exhaustion of populaces, risking the maintainability of fisheries. Carrying out compelling fisheries the board measures, like standards and shut seasons, is critical to address overfishing.

Bycatch and Disposes of:

Bycatch, the accidental catch of non-target species, and disposes of, the dispose of undesirable catch, are critical difficulties in fisheries. Bycatch can incorporate imperiled species, adolescent fish, and non-designated marine life. Supportable fishing rehearses plan to limit bycatch and lessen disposes of.

Natural surroundings Corruption:

Certain fishing rehearses, like base fishing, can cause natural surroundings corruption by harming ocean bottom environments. Safeguarding fundamental living spaces, carrying out gear changes, and taking on maintainable practices are fundamental for limiting the natural effect of fishing.

Unlawful, Unreported, and Unregulated (IUU) Fishing:

IUU fishing represents a serious danger to fisheries the executives by subverting preservation endeavors and adding to overfishing. Combatting IUU fishing requires worldwide collaboration, further developed observing and reconnaissance, and stricter authorization of guidelines.

Environmental Change Effects:

Environmental change influences fisheries by modifying sea temperatures, flows, and the dispersion of fish species. Changes in ocean levels and sea fermentation further compound the difficulties for both wild catch fisheries and hydroponics. Versatile administration is essential to address the effects of environmental change on fisheries.

Maintainable Fisheries The board:

Fisheries Guidelines and Standards:

Viable fisheries the board depends on guidelines and quantities to control fishing exertion and forestall overexploitation. Setting get limits, executing size limitations, and laying out shut seasons are normal measures to guarantee feasible gathering.

Biological system Based Administration:

Environment based administration thinks about the more extensive biological setting of fisheries. It considers the cooperations between species, environment elements, and the general strength of biological systems. This approach intends to keep up with biological equilibrium while supporting human requirements.

Marine Safeguarded Regions (MPAs):

Laying out Marine Safeguarded Regions is a critical methodology in fisheries the executives. MPAs give asylum to fish populaces, permitting them to develop and recreate without fishing pressure. All around planned MPAs add to the protection of biodiversity and the flexibility of environments.

Mechanical Developments:

Mechanical progressions, like satellite checking, electronic labeling, and information investigation, improve fisheries the executives capacities. These apparatuses empower more precise stock appraisals, constant observing of fishing exercises, and the advancement of science-based administration systems.

Accreditation Projects:

Accreditation programs, for example, those presented by associations like the Marine Stewardship Board (MSC), evaluate and affirm fisheries that meet manageability standards. Purchasers can pursue informed decisions by picking items with maintainability certificates, advancing dependable fishing rehearses.

3.1 Historical perspective of European Lobster fisheries

The European lobster (Homarus gammarus) plays had a huge impact throughout the entire existence of fisheries in Europe, with its double-dealing going back hundreds of years. This investigation digs into the authentic point of view of European lobster fisheries, following the development of fishing rehearses, social importance, and the effect of evolving financial circumstances on lobster populaces after some time.

Early Abuse and Social Importance:

Old and Archaic Periods:

Lobsters have been reaped for food and exchange since antiquated times. In archaic Europe, lobsters were plentiful along shorelines, and their accessibility added to the eating regimen of seaside networks. The utilization of straightforward snares and hand gathering strategies denoted the beginning phases of lobster fishing.

Culinary Status and Illustrious Dinners:

Lobsters were at first thought to be a low-status food and were much of the time took care of to workers or detainees. Notwithstanding, their culinary status changed after some time, particularly during the Renaissance. By the seventeenth 100 years, lobsters acquired ubiquity among the high societies, and they turned into a component of sumptuous dinners and blowouts.

Commercialization and Exchange:

With the advancement of nautical and shipping lanes, lobsters turned out to be essential for worldwide business. European lobster fisheries started to supply nearby business sectors as well as exchange networks that arrived at across the mainland. The interest for lobster as a delicacy added to its commercialization.

Mechanical Advances and Industrialization:

eighteenth and nineteenth Hundreds of years:

The eighteenth and nineteenth hundreds of years saw mechanical progressions in fishing strategies. Lobster pots, or traps, turned out to be more complex, taking into consideration more effective lobster gathering. Industrialization likewise prompted the development of fishing networks and the foundation of lobster fisheries as reasonable financial endeavors.

Effect of Steam and Refrigeration:

The presentation of steam-controlled vessels in the nineteenth century changed lobster fishing. Steamships expanded the reach and proficiency of lobster armadas, empowering the extension of fisheries into more profound waters. Refrigeration innovation further broadened the span of lobster markets, considering longer transportation distances.

Guidelines and Protection Endeavors:

As lobster fisheries extended, concerns emerged about overfishing and declining lobster populaces. Accordingly, different European nations executed guidelines to oversee lobster fisheries. Least size limits, occasional terminations, and authorizing frameworks were acquainted with guarantee maintainable practices and safeguard rearing stocks.

Wars and Financial Effect:

Effect of Universal Conflicts:

The two Universal Conflicts significantly affected European lobster fisheries. During seasons of contention, fishing exercises were disturbed, and the financial states of fishing networks were fundamentally affected. Post-war recreation endeavors included drives to revamp and modernize fishing armadas.

Financial Difficulties:

Fishing people group that relied upon lobster fisheries confronted financial difficulties, remembering vacillations for market interest, contest among fishers, and the need to adjust to evolving guidelines. The flexibility of these networks assumed a vital part in the endurance and variation of lobster fisheries.

Ecological Changes and Preservation Difficulties:

Ecological Debasement:

The last 50% of the twentieth century saw expanded familiarity with natural issues, including living space corruption and contamination. Lobster populaces confronted difficulties from changes in water quality, loss of territory, and the effect of human exercises on seaside biological systems.

Infection and Parasites:

Lobster fisheries in Europe have additionally battled with illnesses and parasites influencing lobster populaces. The spread of infections, like shell sickness, and the presence of parasites have had suggestions for the strength of lobster stocks and have required exploration and the executives endeavors.

Protection Measures:

Perceiving the requirement for preservation, European nations have executed different measures to safeguard lobster populaces. Preservation systems incorporate living space rebuilding, marine safeguarded regions, and progressing exploration to more readily grasp the science and biology of European lobsters.

Present day Fisheries The executives and Worldwide Coordinated effort:

European Association Strategies:

With the foundation of the European Association (EU), fisheries the executives turned into a cooperative exertion among part states. Normal Fisheries Strategy (CFP) measures were acquainted with direct fishing exercises, set quantities, and advance feasible practices. Lobster fisheries went under the umbrella of these arrangements.

Cooperative Exploration Drives:

Global coordinated effort in lobster research has become progressively significant. Joint endeavors to concentrate on lobster science, relocation examples, and populace elements add to the advancement of successful administration techniques. Research likewise assumes a part in tending to arising difficulties, for example, the effects of environmental change on lobster territories.

Local area Based Approaches:

Local area based ways to deal with fisheries the board have acquired noticeable quality. Including neighborhood networks in dynamic cycles, taking into account customary information, and advancing manageable fishing rehearses add to the drawn out suitability of lobster fisheries.

Difficulties and Future Viewpoint:

Environmental Change and Sea Fermentation:

Lobster fisheries face difficulties related with environmental change, including climbing ocean temperatures and sea fermentation. These ecological changes can influence lobster territories, prey accessibility, and by and large populace wellbeing. Transformation procedures are pivotal for moderating the impacts of environmental change on European lobster fisheries.

Maintainable Practices and Confirmation:

The significance of maintainable practices in lobster fisheries has turned into a point of convergence. Certificate programs, like those given by the Marine Stewardship Board (MSC), expect to perceive and elevate fisheries that stick to supportability rules. Customers progressively look for reasonably obtained fish, affecting business sector elements.

Adjusting Preservation and Monetary Interests:

Accomplishing a harmony between preservation endeavors and financial interests stays a test. Lobster fisheries are financially huge for the vast majority beach front networks, and tracking down approaches to reasonably deal with these fisheries while supporting occupations requires cautious thought and joint effort.

3.2 Economic significance and commercial value

The financial importance and business worth of different areas assume a crucial part in molding worldwide economies, affecting exchange elements, and affecting the livelihoods of millions. This investigation digs into the multi-layered components of financial importance and business esteem across different enterprises, underlining their commitments to Gross domestic product, work, advancement, and the general success of countries.

Farming and Agribusiness:

Worldwide Food Creation:

Farming structures the foundation of numerous economies, contributing essentially to worldwide food creation. Yields, animals, and fisheries are basic parts of agribusiness, supporting human populaces and supporting food security.

Work and Provincial Jobs:

The horticultural area is a significant boss, particularly in non-industrial nations. It gives vocations to a great many individuals participated in cultivating, fishing, and related exercises. The financial importance reaches out past food creation to incorporate agro-handling ventures.

Advancement in AgTech:

Agribusiness has seen significant development, driven by headways in horticultural innovation (AgTech). Accuracy cultivating, hereditary designing, and feasible practices add to expanded yields, asset proficiency, and strength despite environmental change.

Worldwide Exchange Horticultural Items:

The worldwide exchange of horticultural items is a crucial part of the worldwide economy. Nations spend significant time in the development of specific harvests or animals, taking part in exchange to satisfy homegrown needs and profit by relative benefits.

Fabricating and Modern Creation:

Commitment to Gross domestic product:

Fabricating and modern areas contribute altogether to the Gross domestic product of countries. The development of merchandise, going from autos to gadgets, energizes financial development, makes esteem added items, and produces income.

Work in Assembling:

Fabricating enterprises are significant managers, extending to a different scope of employment opportunities across various expertise levels. Processing plants and creation offices give work amazing open doors that help metropolitan and provincial networks.

Mechanical Headways in Industry 4.0:

The coming of Industry 4.0, described via computerization, information trade, and brilliant advancements, has upset assembling. Advanced mechanics, man-made reasoning, and the Web of Things (IoT) upgrade proficiency, decrease costs, and further develop item quality.

Worldwide Stockpile Chains:

Fabricating is profoundly incorporated into worldwide stockpile chains, with parts and completed items navigating borders. Economic alliance, planned operations, and effective production network the executives are basic for the seriousness of assembling ventures.

Innovation and Data Innovation (IT):

Computerized Change:

The innovation area, especially IT, has been a main impetus behind the computerized change of social orders and economies. The improvement of programming, equipment, and computerized administrations has reshaped the manner in which organizations work and people cooperate.

Development and New companies:

Innovation encourages advancement, leading to new companies and problematic advancements. From Silicon Valley to arising tech center points around the world, new companies add to financial development, work creation, and the ceaseless advancement of the tech scene.

Online business and Computerized Economy:

Online business and the computerized economy have become huge supporters of monetary movement. Online retail, computerized administrations, and the gig economy address new roads of business esteem creation.

Network safety and Information Security:

As innovation assumes an inexorably focal part, the significance of network safety and information security couldn't possibly be more significant. The business benefit of getting advanced resources and guaranteeing information protection has developed couple with the computerized scene.

Money and Banking:

Monetary Administrations and Gross domestic product Commitment:

The money and banking area is a foundation of monetary frameworks, adding to Gross domestic product through different monetary administrations. Banking, venture, protection, and capital business sectors are necessary parts of this area.

Work Creation and Expert Administrations:

Money and banking give a wide exhibit of open positions, going from retail banking to speculation banking and monetary counseling. Experts in finance assume basic parts in overseeing capital, working with ventures, and guaranteeing monetary security.

Job in Financial Turn of events:

The accessibility of monetary administrations is significant for financial turn of events. Admittance to credit, venture capital, and monetary instruments empowers organizations to extend, develop, and add to financial development.

Guideline and Chance Administration:

The money area works inside a structure of guidelines intended to keep up with steadiness and safeguard customers. Risk the executives works on, including administrative consistence and monetary oversight, assume a key part in guaranteeing the strength of monetary organizations.

The travel industry and Neighborliness:

The travel industry as an Income Generator:

The travel industry and cordiality industry is a significant wellspring of income for some nations. Traveler consumptions on convenience, transportation, eating, and attractions contribute straightforwardly to nearby and public economies.

Work Creation and Administration Economy:

The travel industry is a huge boss, giving position in lodgings, eateries, travel services, and related administrations. The business' administration situated nature adds to the improvement of a help economy.

Social and Legacy Worth:

The travel industry frequently features social and legacy locales, enhancing an objective. Verifiable milestones, normal miracles, and one of a kind social encounters become monetary resources as they draw in guests.

Difficulties and Supportability:

While the travel industry brings financial advantages, it additionally acts difficulties such like natural effect, social commodification, and irregularity. Feasible the travel industry rehearses expect to offset monetary additions with ecological and social conservation.

Energy and Normal Assets:

Energy Creation and Utilization:

The energy area is a key part of financial movement, driving businesses, homes, and transportation. The creation and utilization of energy assets, including petroleum products, environmentally friendly power, and atomic power, shape monetary scenes.

Work in Extractive Ventures:

Extractive businesses, like oil and gas extraction and mining, give work valuable open doors. These businesses add to provincial turn of events yet in addition face difficulties connected with ecological effect and asset consumption.

Sustainable power Change:

The change to sustainable power sources, driven by natural worries and innovative progressions, is reshaping the energy area. Sun oriented, wind, hydro, and geothermal power add to maintainable monetary turn of events.

Worldwide Ware Markets:

Regular assets, including minerals, metals, and horticultural products, are exchanged on worldwide business sectors. Item costs impact monetary circumstances, exchange adjusts, and the financial strength of asset rich countries.

Land and Development:

Land as a Resource:

Land, including private, business, and modern properties, addresses a critical resource class. Property proprietorship and land improvement add to privately invested money and financial development.

Development Industry and Occupation Creation:

The development business assumes an essential part in foundation improvement, making position and animating financial action. Private and business development projects add to metropolitan turn of events and restoration.

Real estate Market and Financial Pointers:

The real estate market is firmly checked as a monetary pointer. Vacillations in lodging costs, contract rates, and development action give experiences into more extensive monetary patterns.

Land Speculation and Returns:

Land speculation, whether through property possession, land venture trusts (REITs), or advancement projects, offers expected returns and enhancement valuable open doors for financial backers.

Medical care and Biotechnology:

Medical care Administrations and Consumption:

The medical care area offers fundamental types of assistance and is a huge part of government and confidential consumptions. Clinical consideration, drugs, and wellbeing related enterprises add to financial movement.

Biotechnology and Clinical Development:

Biotechnology has arisen as a driver of clinical development, adding to the improvement of new medications, treatments, and clinical innovations. The biotech business assumes a significant part in further developing medical care results.

Work Creation and Exploration:

Medical care and biotechnology areas set out work open doors in different fields, including medication, nursing, research, and biomanufacturing. Innovative work exercises add to logical progressions.

Worldwide Wellbeing Difficulties and Pandemics:

Worldwide wellbeing challenges, including pandemics, highlight the interconnectedness of medical care frameworks. Reactions to wellbeing emergencies have financial ramifications, affecting general wellbeing spending and medical care foundation.

3.3 Sustainable fisheries management practices

Reasonable fisheries the executives is a basic way to deal with balance the natural soundness of marine biological systems with the monetary and social necessities of networks subject to fisheries assets. This investigation dives into the multi-layered components of economical fisheries the executives works on, going from administrative systems and preservation measures to local area commitment and mechanical developments.

Underpinnings of Supportable Fisheries The board:

Environment Based Administration:

Supportable fisheries the board embraces a biological system based approach, perceiving the interconnectedness of species, natural surroundings, and ecological variables. Biological system based administration considers the more extensive environmental setting to keep up with the wellbeing and versatility of marine biological systems.

Preparatory Standard:

The preparatory standard is a fundamental idea directing reasonable fisheries the board. It advocates for careful steps even with vulnerability, accentuating the need to stay away from possible damage to the marine climate and target species.

Logical Exploration and Information Assortment:

Powerful logical examination and information assortment are foundations of reasonable fisheries the executives. Fisheries researchers evaluate fish stocks, screen environment elements, and examine the effect of fishing exercises. Exact information illuminates the board choices and guarantees the supportability of designated species.

Administrative Structures and Strategy Measures:

Amounts and Catch Cutoff points:

Laying out get portions and cutoff points is a vital administrative measure to forestall overfishing. Fisheries supervisors set logically educated limits on the sum regarding fish that can be reaped, guaranteeing that fishing exercises stay inside practical levels.

Least Size Cutoff points and Stuff Guidelines:

Least size limits for collected species forestall the catch of adolescent fish, permitting them to arrive at conceptive development. Gear guidelines, for example, network size prerequisites and limitations on horrendous fishing rehearses, add to feasible fisheries by limiting bycatch and environment harm.

Occasional Terminations and Fishing Bans:

Occasional terminations and impermanent fishing bans are executed to safeguard weak species during basic life stages, for example, producing. These actions add to the protection of fish populaces and the support of biological system balance.

Marine Safeguarded Regions (MPAs):

Assigning Marine Safeguarded Regions is a successful methodology for rationing biodiversity and permitting fish populaces to recuperate. MPAs go about as asylums where fishing is confined or denied, giving places of refuge to marine life.

Local area Based Approaches:

Co-The board and Partner Association:

Including neighborhood networks and partners in fisheries the executives is crucial to manageable practices. Co-the executives approaches engage networks to take part in navigation, encouraging a feeling of pride and obligation regarding the assets.

Native Information and Conventional Practices:

Perceiving and incorporating native information and conventional practices into fisheries the executives improves the adequacy of protection endeavors. Native people group frequently have important bits of knowledge into the way of behaving of nearby species and supportable gathering rehearses.

Local area Upheld Fisheries (CSFs):

Local area Upheld Fisheries drives associate purchasers straightforwardly with nearby fishers, advancing supportable practices and guaranteeing fair pay. CSFs upgrade straightforwardness and recognizability in the fish production network, cultivating a nearer connection among fishers and buyers.

Mechanical Developments in Fisheries The board:

Satellite Observing and Reconnaissance:

Satellite innovation empowers constant observing of fishing exercises, assisting specialists with following vessel developments, distinguish unlawful fishing, and authorize guidelines. Satellite information upgrades straightforwardness and responsibility in the fishing business.

Electronic Observing and Detailing:

Electronic observing frameworks on fishing vessels, combined with electronic detailing, give precise information on get organization and fishing exertion. These advancements support science-based navigation and work on the productivity of fisheries the board.

Blockchain and Detectability:

Blockchain innovation is progressively used to lay out detectability in the fish store network. By recording and confirming each step of the store network, from catch to customer, blockchain improves straightforwardness and battles unlawful, unreported, and unregulated (IUU) fishing.

Savvy Fisheries and Information Investigation:

Savvy fisheries use information investigation to survey fish stocks, anticipate drifts, and streamline fishing rehearses. Progressed examination assist with distinguishing designs, survey the effect of ecological factors, and refine the executives procedures for further developed maintainability.

Relieving Natural Effect:

Natural surroundings Security and Rebuilding:

Feasible fisheries the board includes securing and reestablishing fundamental environments. Techniques incorporate keeping away from damaging fishing works on, executing spatial administration gauges, and reestablishing corrupted biological systems to help sound fish populaces.

Diminishing Bycatch and Disposes of:

Bycatch, the unexpected catch of non-target species, and disposes of, the removal of undesirable catch, present critical difficulties. Specific fishing gear, changed fishing strategies, and impetuses to diminish bycatch add to more reasonable fishing rehearses.

Environmental Change Transformation:

Environmental change presents difficulties to fisheries by adjusting sea conditions and affecting the circulation of species. Practical fisheries the board incorporates methodologies for adjusting to changing natural circumstances, for example, moving fishery seasons or changing catch limits.

Affirmation Projects and Market Drives:

Marine Stewardship Board (MSC) Certificate:

The Marine Stewardship Board (MSC) certificate is a generally perceived norm for supportable fisheries. Fisheries that meet MSC standards exhibit adherence to supportable works on, guaranteeing that buyers can pursue informed decisions while buying fish.

Ecolabeling and Eco-Affirmation:

Ecolabeling drives and eco-confirmation programs, past MSC, furnish buyers with extra marks of manageability. These names, upheld by valid guidelines, engage purchasers to help fisheries that focus on natural protection.

Worldwide Participation and Administration:

Local Fisheries The executives Associations (RFMOs):

Worldwide joint effort through RFMOs is vital for overseeing fisheries that range different nations. These associations lay out guidelines, coordinate observing endeavors, and work with agreeable administration to guarantee the maintainability of shared fish stocks.

Joined Countries Show on the Law of the Ocean (UNCLOS):

The UNCLOS gives a lawful system to the preservation and the executives of living marine assets. It lays out the limitations of countries in the utilization of the seas, advancing participation and maintainable practices on a worldwide scale.

Battle Against Unlawful, Unreported, and Unregulated (IUU) Fishing:

Combatting IUU fishing is really important in supportable fisheries the executives. Peaceful accords, port state measures, and agreeable requirement endeavors mean to dispose of unlawful fishing rehearses that compromise the soundness of marine environments.

Difficulties and Future Bearings:

Overcapacity and Appropriations:

Overcapacity in the fishing business, exacerbated by government appropriations, challenges the manageability of worldwide fisheries. Tending to overcapacity requires the decrease of appropriations that add to exorbitant fishing exertion.

Information Lack and Logical Vulnerability:

Information lacks and logical vulnerabilities present difficulties to successful fisheries the executives. Further developing information assortment techniques, improving exploration endeavors, and putting resources into observing advancements are fundamental for tending to information holes.

Social and Financial Effects:

Carrying out supportable fisheries the executives rehearses should think about the social and monetary effects on fishing networks. Progressing to additional reasonable practices may at first influence jobs, needing help and transformation procedures for impacted partners.

Environmental Change and Sea Fermentation:

The effects of environmental change and sea fermentation on marine biological systems add intricacy to maintainable fisheries the board. Procedures for adjusting to changing natural circumstances and relieving environment related influences are basic for long haul maintainability.

Chapter 4

Conservation Challenges And Efforts

Preservation, the proactive and conscious work to safeguard and reasonably deal with Earth's biodiversity, is confronting phenomenal difficulties in the advanced time. As human exercises keep on influencing environments, progressives are defied with a huge number of dangers that require inventive and cooperative arrangements. This investigation digs into the intricacies of protection challenges, going from territory misfortune and environmental change to poaching and contamination, and inspects the assorted endeavors being made worldwide to shield the planet's rich woven artwork of life.

Territory Misfortune and Fracture:

Deforestation and Urbanization:

Maybe the most unavoidable test to biodiversity protection is living space misfortune. Deforestation, driven by agrarian development, logging, and urbanization, upsets environments and uproots innumerable species. The transformation of normal natural surroundings into farming fields and metropolitan scenes pieces environments, confining populaces and lessening hereditary variety.

Influence on Cornerstone Species:

Living space misfortune excessively influences cornerstone species — creatures that to a great extent affect their current circumstance. The vanishing of cornerstone species can set off flowing impacts, undermining whole environments. Safeguarding the territories of these basic species is principal for keeping up with environmental equilibrium.

Land Use Arranging and Safeguarded Regions:

Compelling area use arranging is an essential part of preservation endeavors. Laying out and keeping up with safeguarded regions, like public stops and holds, gives shelters to assorted species. Nonetheless, adjusting human requirements for improvement with the basic to safeguard normal natural surroundings is a steady test.

Environmental Change and A dangerous atmospheric devation:

Changes in Territories and Species Reaches:

Environmental change is modifying temperature and precipitation designs, prompting shifts in natural surroundings and the scopes of numerous species. A few animal groups might battle to adjust or relocate to reasonable conditions, seriously endangering them of termination. Environment actuated changes additionally influence the planning of key life altering situations, like movement and multiplication.

Sea Fermentation and Coral Fading:

The seas, significant for biodiversity, are defenseless against environmental change influences. Sea fermentation, a consequence of expanded carbon dioxide ingestion, represents a danger to marine life, especially organic entities with calcium carbonate shells or skeletons. Coral blanching, driven by increasing ocean temperatures, jeopardizes coral reef environments, influencing various marine species.

Protection Techniques in an Evolving Environment:

Adjusting protection techniques to a changing environment is basic. This incorporates laying out environment strong safeguarded regions, carrying out territory rebuilding projects, and elevating scene network to help species in moving their reaches. Environment savvy protection arranging is fundamental for defending biodiversity despite progressing a dangerous atmospheric devation.

Overexploitation and Poaching:

Unlawful Untamed life Exchange:

The unlawful untamed life exchange stays a huge danger to numerous species, driving populaces toward termination. Poaching for things, for example, ivory, rhino horns, and fascinating pets keeps on devastating populaces, adding to the decay of famous species like elephants and rhinoceroses.

Impractical Fishing Practices:

Overfishing and damaging fishing rehearses present serious dangers to marine biodiversity. Impractical works on, including base fishing and bycatch, exhaust target fish populaces as well as mischief non-target species and harm delicate marine living spaces.

Hunting and Bushmeat Exchange:

Chasing after bushmeat, driven by means requirements and business interests, represents a danger to earthbound animal categories, especially in tropical locales. Impractical hunting can upset food networks, adjust biological elements, and lead to the decay of weak species.

Preservation through Requirement and Local area Commitment:

Protection endeavors tending to overexploitation require a multi-layered approach. Reinforcing policing battle unlawful natural life exchange, advancing maintainable fishing rehearses, and drawing in neighborhood networks in preservation drives are basic procedures. Local area based protection projects that give elective vocations can assist with diminishing dependence on exercises that hurt biodiversity.

Contamination and Ecological Corruption:

Plastic Contamination and Marine Flotsam and jetsam:

Plastic contamination is an unavoidable ecological test influencing marine biological systems. A great many lots of plastic waste enter seas every year, hurting marine life through ingestion, ensnarement, and living space debasement. Moderating plastic contamination requires worldwide endeavors to decrease plastic utilization and work on squander the board.

Synthetic Contamination and Living space Pollution:

Synthetic poisons, including pesticides, composts, and modern synthetic compounds, defile environments, influencing soil, water, and air quality. These contaminations can have flowing consequences for species, upsetting conceptive and formative cycles and compromising the soundness of whole environments.

Air Contamination and its Natural Effects:

Air contamination, including toxins like sulfur dioxide and nitrogen oxides, has far reaching environmental effects. Corrosive downpour, an outcome of air contamination, hurts sea-going biological systems, harms vegetation, and disintegrates soil. Tending to air contamination requires global participation and complete arrangements to lessen discharges.

Preservation Methodologies for Contamination Moderation:

Preservation endeavors pointed toward relieving contamination include both administrative measures and public mindfulness crusades. Stricter ecological guidelines, supportable rural practices, and waste decrease drives add to lessening contamination. Schooling and promotion assume vital parts in cultivating a more extensive comprehension of the effects of contamination on biodiversity.

Obtrusive Species and Biotic Homogenization:

Presentation of Non-Local Species:

The presentation of non-local species, whether purposefully or inadvertently, can unfavorably affect nearby environments. Obtrusive species may outcompete local verdure, prompting declines or terminations of native species.

Biotic Homogenization and Loss of Biodiversity:

Obtrusive species add to biotic homogenization — the interaction by which nearby species arrays become more comparable after some time. This homogenization lessens in general biodiversity and debilitates biological system versatility to aggravations.

Early Location and Quick Reaction:

Early location of intrusive species and quick reaction measures are indispensable for forestalling their foundation and spread. Vigorous biosecurity measures at ports and boundaries, alongside state funded schooling, are fundamental parts of obtrusive species the executives.

Illness and Arising Dangers:

Illness Transmission in Natural life Populaces:

Illness flare-ups in untamed life populaces can significantly affect biodiversity. Arising irresistible infections, frequently worked with by human exercises and worldwide travel, can prompt populace declines and upset environmental associations.

Land and water proficient Chytrid Organism and Bat White-Nose Disorder:

Explicit sicknesses, for example, the land and water proficient chytrid parasite and bat white-nose condition, have devastatingly affected weak species. These sicknesses have added to populace declines and modified natural elements in impacted environments.

One Wellbeing Approach:

Embracing a One Wellbeing approach, which perceives the interconnectedness of human, creature, and ecological wellbeing, is pivotal for tending to infection related protection challenges. This includes cooperative endeavors between progressives, general wellbeing authorities, and veterinarians to comprehend and oversee sickness elements in an all encompassing way.

Protection Examples of overcoming adversity and Positive Drives:

Species Recuperation Projects:

Various species recuperation programs have exhibited outcome in forestalling terminations and remaking populaces. Models incorporate the California condor, the dark footed ferret, and the Middle Eastern oryx. These projects include hostage rearing, living space rebuilding, and renewed introduction endeavors.

Safeguarded Regions and Protection Stores:

The foundation and successful administration of safeguarded regions and protection holds play had a crucial impact in saving biodiversity. Very much oversaw stops and saves give places of refuge to different species, permitting them to flourish and adding to generally speaking biological system wellbeing.

Local area Based Protection Activities:

Drawing in nearby networks in preservation projects has demonstrated viable in accomplishing maintainable results. Local area based drives that adjust protection objectives to neighborhood needs, like economical asset the board and ecotourism, encourage a feeling of stewardship and backing for biodiversity.

Innovation and Protection Advancements:

Mechanical advancements, including camera traps, satellite following, and DNA investigation, have altered protection endeavors. These devices give important bits of knowledge into untamed life conduct, movement examples, and populace elements, empowering more designated and compelling preservation procedures.

4.1 Conservation status of European Lobster populations

The European lobster (Homarus gammarus) holds biological, financial, and social importance in the seaside districts it occupies. As a cornerstone animal types, it assumes a vital part in keeping up with marine biological system balance, and its business esteem has made it an objective for fishing exercises all through its reach. This investigation digs into the preservation status of European lobster populaces, analyzing the elements affecting their overflow, the difficulties they face, continuous protection endeavors, and the significance of maintainable administration to guarantee their drawn out practicality.

Science and Nature of the European Lobster:

Life Cycle and Generation:

The existence pattern of the European lobster is mind boggling and ranges a few formative stages. In the wake of bring forth from eggs, hatchlings go through a progression of sheds prior to settling to the sea floor as adolescents. Lobsters proceed to shed and develop all through their lives, arriving at sexual development at around 5-7 years. Multiplication includes a romance custom, mating, and egg-conveying by females. The eggs hatch into hatchlings, going full circle.

Territory Inclinations:

European lobsters possess different beach front conditions, from rough shores to sandy bottoms. They look for cover in fissure and tunnels during the day and arise around evening time to scrounge for prey. The accessibility of reasonable concealing spots is pivotal for their endurance.

Taking care of Propensities and Job in Biological systems:

European lobsters are pioneering omnivores, consuming a fluctuated diet that incorporates little fish, mollusks, scavangers, and debris. As hunters, they assist with directing the populaces of their prey, adding to the general soundness of marine environments. The unpredictable cooperations among lobsters and their current circumstance feature their environmental significance.

Authentic Points of view on European Lobster Fisheries:

Culinary Delicacy and Noble Imagery:

The European lobster has a rich culinary history, with specifies tracing all the way back to old civic establishments. During bygone eras, lobsters became images of richness and were highlighted in imperial dining experiences. Their prominence as an extravagance food thing continued as the centuries progressed, adding to their financial worth.

Customary Fishing Practices:

Before the industrialization of fisheries, lobster collecting depended on customary and distinctive techniques. Waterfront people group created traps and pots to catch lobsters, with rehearses frequently went down through ages. These techniques mirrored a maintainable way to deal with lobster fishing, permitting populaces to normally renew.

Industrialization and Innovative Advances:

The late nineteenth and mid twentieth hundreds of years saw huge changes in lobster fisheries with the approach of industrialization. Steam-fueled vessels, more effective snares, and further developed transportation worked with the extension of lobster fishing exercises. The worldwide interest for lobster as a delicacy drove the improvement of commodity markets.

Worries of Overexploitation and Protection Measures:

As lobster fisheries extended, worries about overexploitation arose. Strengthened fishing endeavors, territory corruption, and ecological changes added to decreases in lobster populaces. Preservation measures, including size limits, get amounts, and occasional terminations, were acquainted with safeguard and oversee lobster stocks.

Current Preservation Status:

Populace Declines and Overfishing Concerns:

European lobster populaces have confronted decreases in different areas, raising worries about overfishing. The blend of expanded request, environment corruption, and environment related factors has added to variances in lobster overflow. Logical evaluations are significant for figuring out populace elements and illuminating preservation systems.

Provincial Varieties:

The preservation status of European lobster populaces fluctuates across districts. While certain areas have seen declines and increased preservation endeavors, others have carried out fruitful administration practices to keep up with feasible stocks. Understanding the elements affecting these varieties is fundamental for designated protection measures.

Hereditary Variety and Flexibility:

Keeping up with hereditary variety inside lobster populaces is vital for their drawn out strength. Inbreeding and hereditary homogeneity can make populaces more defenseless to sicknesses and natural changes. Protection techniques ought to consider the hereditary strength of lobster populaces as a critical calculate guaranteeing their versatile limit.

Protection Difficulties:

Natural surroundings Corruption and Misfortune:

Natural surroundings corruption, including waterfront improvement, contamination, and the effects of environmental change, represents a critical danger to lobster living spaces. Loss of reasonable concealing spots, fundamental for their endurance, can prompt expanded death rates and decreased conceptive achievement.

Environmental Change Effects:

The warming of sea temperatures and other environment related changes present difficulties to European lobster populaces. These progressions can impact their dissemination, generation, and shedding designs. Understanding and relieving the effects of environmental change are basic parts of lobster protection.

Connections with Fishing Stuff:

The utilization of specific fishing gear, especially those with non-particular qualities, represents a danger to lobster populaces. Base fishing and other horrendous practices can harm natural surroundings, trap non-target species, and add to overfishing. Manageable fishing rehearses that limit adverse consequences on lobster populaces are fundamental.

Unlawful Fishing and Authorization:

Unlawful, unreported, and unregulated (IUU) fishing exercises present a test to powerful lobster protection. Absence of implementation and observing can prompt overharvesting and unlawful exchange. Reinforcing administrative systems and further developing reconnaissance are vital for fighting IUU fishing.

Protection Endeavors and The executives Techniques:

Size Cutoff points and Least Legitimate Sizes:

Executing size cutoff points and least lawful sizes for gathered lobsters is a typical administration system. These guidelines plan to safeguard adolescent lobsters, permitting them to arrive at development prior to being caught. Size limits add to manageable reaping rehearses.

Portions and Catch Cutoff points:

Setting standards and catch limits is a critical part of practical fisheries the board. By managing how much lobster that can be collected, specialists can forestall overfishing and guarantee that populaces have the chance to recharge. Science-based evaluations advise the foundation regarding fitting shares.

Occasional Terminations and Fishing Bans:

Occasional terminations and transitory fishing bans are carried out to safeguard lobsters during basic life stages, like shedding and generation. These actions take into consideration populace recuperation and add to the general manageability of lobster fisheries.

Marine Safeguarded Regions (MPAs):

Laying out Marine Safeguarded Regions (MPAs) can make asylum regions where lobsters are protected from fishing exercises. MPAs add to biodiversity protection, give living spaces to different species, and act as hotspots for renewing encompassing regions.

Living space Reclamation and Upgrade:

Living space reclamation projects expect to restore debased lobster environments. This can include making counterfeit designs that imitate regular concealing spots or reestablishing seaside biological systems to give reasonable conditions to adolescent and grown-up lobsters.

Local area Based Administration:

Including neighborhood networks in the administration of lobster fisheries upgrades the viability of protection endeavors. Local area based approaches engage partners to partake in dynamic cycles, cultivating a feeling of obligation for the manageable utilization of lobster assets.

Mechanical Advancements in Lobster Preservation:

Satellite Following and Information Assortment:

Satellite following innovation permits researchers to screen lobster developments and conduct. Information gathered through satellite following add to understanding movement designs, living space use, and the effect of natural changes on lobster populaces.

Hereditary Observing and Populace Studies:

Hereditary observing gives bits of knowledge into the variety and soundness of lobster populaces. Populace studies, including hereditary investigations, assist with surveying the effect of fishing exercises, recognize unmistakable populaces, and illuminate preservation systems that protect hereditary variety.

Remote Detecting and Living space Planning:

Remote detecting advances and natural surroundings planning add to the ID and observing of basic lobster environments. Understanding the spatial dispersion of lobsters and their favored natural surroundings is fundamental for executing viable protection measures.

Hydroponics and Stock Improvement:

Lobster hydroponics and stock improvement programs offer likely answers for supplement wild populaces. Controlled raising in hydroponics offices can give a wellspring of lobsters to deliver into the wild, supporting populace recuperation endeavors.

Public Mindfulness and Partner Commitment:

Instructive Missions:

Public mindfulness and training efforts assume a fundamental part in advancing reasonable lobster preservation. These missions illuminate people in general about the significance regarding lobster biological systems, the difficulties they face, and the job people can play in supporting protection endeavors.

Partner Cooperation:

Cooperation among partners, including government offices, fisheries the executives associations, researchers, and industry delegates, is fundamental for compelling lobster preservation. Drawing in different partners cultivates an aggregate obligation to maintainable practices and works with the trading of information and skill.

Confirmation Projects and Eco-marking:

Confirmation programs, like the Marine Stewardship Board (MSC), give eco-marks to reasonably gathered fish, including lobster. Eco-marking permits shoppers to pursue informed decisions, supporting fisheries that stick to naturally mindful practices.

4.2 Threats to their survival

The European lobster (Homarus gammarus) faces a heap of dangers that imperil its endurance in nature. This notorious marine species, esteemed for its natural job and monetary importance, faces difficulties going from overfishing and living space corruption to environmental change and arising infections. This investigation dives into the multi-layered dangers that European lobster populaces experience, breaking down the interconnected elements that add to their weakness and looking at expected answers for guaranteeing their drawn out endurance.

Overfishing and Abuse:

Verifiable Overharvesting:

European lobsters have a long history of double-dealing, going back hundreds of years when they were viewed as a delicacy for blue-bloods. Overharvesting, driven by the appeal for lobster meat, has generally drained populaces in different districts. The power of fishing endeavors expanded essentially with industrialization and the advancement of more proficient fishing innovations.

Unregulated Fishing Practices:

Unregulated and impractical fishing rehearses represent a huge danger to lobster populaces. The shortfall of clear rules or requirement measures can prompt over the top reaping, particularly during periods when lobsters are more defenseless, for example, during shedding or conceptive stages. Uncontrolled fishing strain can drain stocks and upset populace elements.

Bycatch and Non-Specific Fishing Stuff:

Non-specific fishing gear, including particular kinds of traps and fishes, can prompt bycatch of small lobsters and other non-target species. Bycatch adds to death rates among adolescent lobsters, disturbing age-class structures and obstructing populace recuperation. The utilization of more specific stuff is urgent for limiting these adverse consequences.

Unlawful, Unreported, and Unregulated (IUU) Fishing:

IUU fishing worsens the dangers presented by overfishing. Unlawful exercises, including the unlawful reap of small lobsters, surpass laid out amounts, and unreported gets, add to the corruption of lobster populaces. Reinforcing administrative systems, improving observing, and expanding punishments for criminal operations are fundamental for combatting IUU fishing.

Natural surroundings Debasement and Misfortune:

Seaside Improvement:

Urbanization and seaside advancement adjust regular living spaces basic for European lobsters. The development of harbors, marinas, and framework can prompt the obliteration of rough substrates and concealing spots fundamental for lobsters to avoid hunters and track down cover during sunshine hours.

Contamination and Pollutants:

Contamination from different sources, including modern releases, farming spill-over, and metropolitan overflow, brings impurities into lobster natural surroundings. Substance poisons can antagonistically influence lobster wellbeing, upsetting shedding processes, weakening regenerative abilities, and adding to populace declines.

Digging and Base Fishing:

Digging and base fishing rehearses, frequently connected with business fishing exercises, can make actual harm the seabed and annihilate lobster territories. These exercises disturb the construction of the sea depths, eliminating fundamental concealing spots and adversely affecting the general soundness of marine environments.

Environment Related Changes:

Environmental change acquaints extra stressors with lobster living spaces. Climbing ocean temperatures, sea fermentation, and changes in sea flows can impact the dispersion of prey species and adjust the accessibility of appropriate territories for lobsters. Understanding and relieving the effects of environment related changes are basic for the drawn out endurance of lobster populaces.

Environmental Change Effects:

Temperature-Subordinate Life Cycles:

The existence pattern of European lobsters is intently attached to temperature. Hotter waters can impact shedding examples, generation, and by and large metabolic cycles. Changes in sea temperatures might disturb the synchronization of these basic life altering situations, influencing the endurance and wellness of lobster populaces.

Changes in Prey Accessibility:

Environmental change can modify the overflow and dispersion of prey species that structure the eating routine of European lobsters. Changes in the accessibility of reasonable prey can affect lobster development rates, propagation, and generally populace wellbeing. Understanding the complex connections among lobsters and their prey is fundamental for anticipating and alleviating environment initiated influences.

Sea Fermentation:

Sea fermentation, an outcome of expanded carbon dioxide ingestion via seawater, represents a danger to marine creatures with calcium carbonate skeletons or shells. While lobsters themselves are not straightforwardly impacted, fermentation can influence their prey and upset food networks, possibly influencing the general soundness of lobster populaces.

Ocean Level Ascent and Living space Movements:

Rising ocean levels and natural surroundings shifts impact the dissemination of seaside environments. Lobsters depend on unambiguous natural surroundings for haven, proliferation, and rummaging. Changes in the design and accessibility of these territories because of ocean level ascent can prompt relocation and expanded weakness to predation.

Illness and Wellbeing Difficulties:

Arising Illnesses:

Lobsters, in the same way as other marine species, can be vulnerable to arising sicknesses. Microbes and parasites, already unencountered or not considered huge, can present dangers to lobster populaces. Sickness flare-ups can prompt expanded death rates, influencing the overflow and construction of lobster populaces.

Stress from Ecological Changes:

Ecological stressors, including contamination, natural surroundings corruption, and temperature vacillations, can think twice about safe frameworks of lobsters. Debilitated resistant reactions make them more helpless to sicknesses and diminish their capacity to adapt to changing ecological circumstances.

Anthropogenic Stressors:

Human exercises add to stressors that influence lobster wellbeing. Commotion contamination, for instance, from transportation and submerged development exercises, can upset lobster conduct and stress their physiological frameworks. Understanding the combined effects of different stressors is essential for relieving their consequences for lobster populaces.

Obtrusive Species and Contest:

Presentation of Non-Local Species:

The presentation of non-local species can upset local environments and effect lobster populaces. Obtrusive species might contend with lobsters for food and territory, prompting changes in populace elements and the general design of marine networks.

Biotic Homogenization:

Biotic homogenization, the interaction by which biological systems become more comparative because of the predominance of a couple of animal varieties, can result from the presentation of intrusive species. In the event that non-local species outcompete or go after local species, including lobsters, it can prompt a decrease in by and large biodiversity and environment strength.

Predation and Ruthless Tensions:

Changes in hunter prey elements can influence lobster endurance. The presentation of new hunters or changes in the wealth of existing hunters can increment predation pressures on lobster populaces. Understanding these elements is pivotal for anticipating and moderating predation-related dangers.

Human-Untamed life Struggle:

Cooperations with Fisheries:

While fisheries are a critical wellspring of anthropogenic dangers, cooperations with lobster fisheries can prompt contentions. The opposition for space and assets among lobsters and fishing activities can bring about expanded death rates, especially during the catching and collecting process.

Trap in Fishing Stuff:

Lobsters are helpless to trap in fishing gear, particularly when non-specific strategies are utilized. Entanglement in traps or fish nets can cause wounds, stress, and mortality. Further developing stuff selectivity and carrying out measures to decrease snare risk are fundamental for limiting these contentions.

Adjustment to Human Presence:

Adjustment to human presence, particularly in regions with normal fishing exercises, can modify lobster conduct. Acclimated lobsters might turn out to be not so much watchful but rather more helpless to predation. Understanding the social reactions of lobsters to human exercises is critical for creating preservation systems that limit adverse consequences.

Combined and Intuitive Impacts:

Synergistic Effects of Various Stressors:

European lobsters frequently face one, yet various stressors all the while. The combined impacts of overfishing, living space corruption, environmental change, and different dangers can have synergistic effects, enhancing the general weight on lobster populaces and decreasing their versatility.

Intelligent Consequences for Biological system Elements:

The collaborations between lobster populaces and their current circumstance are intricate and interconnected. Changes in lobster overflow and circulation can include flowing consequences for different species inside marine biological systems. Understanding these intelligent impacts is fundamental for anticipating biological system wide results and executing compelling preservation measures.

Preservation Systems and Arrangements:

Economical Fisheries The executives:

Carrying out maintainable fisheries the executives rehearses is basic to tending to overfishing dangers. This incorporates setting and authorizing get limits, laying out size guidelines, and utilizing methods that diminish bycatch. Science-based administration guarantees that collecting rates are inside feasible cutoff points, permitting lobster populaces to recuperate and flourish.

Living space Insurance and Reclamation:

Safeguarding and reestablishing basic lobster territories is fundamental for their endurance. Laying out marine safeguarded regions (MPAs), carrying out living space rebuilding tasks, and managing waterfront improvement are key techniques. These drives give places of refuge to lobsters to shed, imitate, and track down cover.

Environment Versatile Protection:

Creating environment versatile protection techniques includes understanding and adjusting to the effects of environmental change. This might incorporate the production of environment shrewd MPAs, observing temperature-subordinate life processes, and carrying out versatile administration measures to address the unique difficulties presented by an evolving environment.

Illness Checking and Exploration:

Observing and exploring arising sicknesses in lobster populaces are urgent for early identification and the board. Laying out illness observation programs, grasping the natural drivers of infections, and creating methodologies to relieve sickness influences add to the general strength of lobster populaces.

Intrusive Species The executives:

Overseeing intrusive species includes forestalling their presentation, checking their presence, and executing measures to control their effect. Strong biosecurity measures at ports and lines, early recognition programs, and compelling annihilation procedures are indispensable parts of intrusive species the executives.

Local area Commitment and Partner Coordinated effort:

Connecting with neighborhood networks and partners in preservation endeavors is fundamental for progress. Including fishers, researchers, government organizations, and the public encourages a common obligation regarding the reasonable administration of lobster populaces. Local area based approaches, with an accentuation on training and mindfulness, enable partners to add to preservation objectives.

Mechanical Advancements in Fisheries:

Embracing mechanical developments upgrades the accuracy and adequacy of protection endeavors. Satellite following, submerged cameras, and hereditary checking advancements give significant information to grasping lobster conduct, populace elements, and hereditary wellbeing. These devices add to confirm based dynamic in fisheries the board.

Chapter 5

Climate Change Impacts And Adaptations

Environmental change, driven by human exercises like consuming petroleum products, deforestation, and modern cycles, is changing the World's environment at a phenomenal rate. These progressions have significant ramifications for environments, social orders, and economies around the world. In this investigation, we dive into the complex effects of environmental change and the vital variations expected to explore a quickly impacting world. From climbing temperatures and ocean level changes to shifts in precipitation designs and the strengthening of outrageous climate occasions, the difficulties presented by environmental change are different and require creative arrangements.

1. **Effects of Environmental Change:**

Climbing Temperatures:

Worldwide temperatures have been consistently ascending because of the collection of ozone depleting substances in the environment. This warming pattern has sweeping outcomes, impacting weather conditions, softening ice covers and glacial masses, and modifying biological systems. In earthly conditions, higher temperatures can prompt changes in vegetation, disturbances in natural life environments, and changes in the dispersion of species.

Ocean Level Ascent:

One of the most noticeable effects of environmental change is the ascent in ocean levels. This peculiarity is basically determined by the warm extension of seawater as it warms and the liquefying of polar ice covers and ice sheets. Rising ocean levels present dangers to waterfront networks, prompting expanded flooding, disintegration, and saltwater interruption into freshwater sources. Low-lying island countries are especially powerless against these changes.

Changing Precipitation Examples:

Environmental change is adjusting worldwide precipitation designs, prompting shifts in the appropriation and force of precipitation. A few locales experience more regular and serious precipitation, prompting flooding and avalanches, while others face delayed dry seasons and water shortage. These progressions have significant ramifications for farming, water assets, and the general versatility of biological systems.

Outrageous Climate Occasions:

The recurrence and force of outrageous climate occasions, including tropical storms, heatwaves, fierce blazes, and floods, are on the ascent. These occasions present critical dangers to human wellbeing, framework, and normal biological systems. The rising recurrence of outrageous occasions intensifies the difficulties of calamity readiness, reaction, and recuperation.

Sea Fermentation:

The ingestion of abundance carbon dioxide by the world's seas is causing sea fermentation. This cycle, frequently alluded to as the "other CO_2 issue," adversely affects marine life, especially creatures with calcium carbonate skeletons or shells, like corals and mollusks. Sea fermentation undermines marine biodiversity, disturbs food networks, and compromises the occupations of networks subject to fisheries.

Biodiversity Misfortune:

Environmental change adds to the deficiency of biodiversity as biological systems face disturbances in temperature, precipitation, and living space accessibility. Species that can't adjust or move rapidly enough might confront populace declines or termination. The deficiency of biodiversity has flowing impacts on biological system capabilities, including fertilization, supplement cycling, and vermin control.

Influence on Horticulture:

Environmental change presents critical difficulties to horticulture, influencing crop yields, animals creation, and food security. Changes in temperature and precipitation examples can prompt changes in appropriate developing regions, modified nuisance and sickness elements, and expanded weakness to outrageous climate occasions. Supportable farming practices and versatile methodologies are fundamental for guaranteeing food creation even with environmental change.

2. **Transformations to Environmental Change:**

Environmentally friendly power Change:

Relieving environmental change requires a progress from petroleum products to sustainable power sources. Sun based, wind, hydroelectric, and geothermal energy offer economical choices that decrease ozone harming substance discharges. Putting resources into environmentally friendly power foundation and advancing energy productivity are critical parts of worldwide endeavors to battle environmental change.

Environment Strong Horticulture:

Environment strong agribusiness includes carrying out rehearses that improve the flexibility of cultivating frameworks to changing climatic circumstances. This incorporates the advancement of dry season open minded crops, further developed water the board methods, agroforestry drives, and the reception of environment savvy rural practices. Manageable agribusiness adds to food security and assists ranchers with adapting to environment related difficulties.

Environment Based Transformation:

Environment put together transformation centers with respect to utilizing normal biological systems to upgrade flexibility to environmental change. Safeguarding and reestablishing backwoods, wetlands, and beach front biological systems offers fundamental types of assistance, for example, flood control, water decontamination, and living space for biodiversity. Biological system based approaches add to both environment transformation and relief.

Environment Strong Framework:

Planning and executing environment versatile framework is fundamental for limiting the effect of outrageous climate occasions and rising ocean levels. This incorporates developing structures that can endure storms and floods, creating productive seepage frameworks, and integrating green foundation arrangements. Environment strong framework shields networks and decreases the financial expenses of environment related calamities.

Water The executives and Protection:

Environmental change influences water accessibility and dissemination, making powerful water the board essential. Carrying out water preservation measures, further developing water-use proficiency, and putting resources into feasible water framework add to environment variation. This is especially significant in locales confronting expanded dry seasons or changes in precipitation designs.

Local area Based Transformation:

Drawing in neighborhood networks in the variation cycle is fundamental for building versatility. Local area based variation includes engaging networks to recognize and carry out techniques that address their particular environment related difficulties. This approach perceives the neighborhood information and skill of networks and guarantees that transformation measures are logically significant.

Environment Savvy Metropolitan Preparation:

Metropolitan regions are defenseless against the effects of environmental change, including heatwaves, flooding, and ocean level ascent. Environment savvy metropolitan arranging includes planning urban communities with supportable foundation, green spaces, and productive transportation frameworks. Integrating environment contemplations into metropolitan advancement lessens the dangers related with environmental change.

Interest in Exploration and Development:

Progressions in examination and advancement assume a urgent part in creating successful environment variation methodologies. Putting resources into environment science, innovation, and imaginative arrangements adds to a superior comprehension of environment influences and the improvement of versatile measures. This remembers research for strong yield assortments, environment demonstrating, and early admonition frameworks for outrageous climate occasions.

3. **Global Participation and Strategy Measures:**

Worldwide Environment Arrangements:

Worldwide participation is fundamental for tending to the worldwide idea of environmental change. Arrangements, for example, the Paris Understanding expect to join nations in their endeavors to restrict worldwide temperature increments and improve environment strength. Responsibilities to decrease ozone depleting substance discharges and backing weak countries are essential for accomplishing aggregate environment objectives.

Environment Money:

Monetary help for environment transformation and moderation estimates in non-industrial nations is a vital part of worldwide environment endeavors. Environment finance helps countries in carrying out reasonable works on, progressing to sustainable power, and adjusting to the effects of environmental change. Assembling environment finance is basic for accomplishing worldwide environment targets.

Carbon Evaluating:

Carbon evaluating instruments, for example, carbon expenses and cap-and-exchange frameworks, give monetary motivators to decrease ozone harming substance outflows. By putting a cost on carbon, these systems urge organizations and ventures to take on cleaner advances and put resources into low-carbon rehearses. Carbon estimating is a market-based way to deal with relieving environmental change.

Innovation Move and Limit Building:

Working with the exchange of environment strong advancements and building the limit of countries to carry out versatile measures are essential parts of global environment collaboration. Created nations can uphold agricultural countries in embracing reasonable works on, upgrading their versatility, and jumping to cleaner advancements.

Nature-Based Arrangements:

Nature-based arrangements include utilizing regular cycles and biological systems to address environment challenges. This incorporates reforestation projects, practical land the board, and the rebuilding of corrupted environments. Nature-based arrangements add to carbon sequestration, biodiversity preservation, and environment transformation.

5.1 Influence of climate change on Atlantic Waters and lobster habitats

Atlantic waters, enveloping the huge scope of the Atlantic Sea, are encountering significant changes driven by environmental change. These adjustments, going from climbing temperatures and moving sea flows to changes in precipitation designs, have significant ramifications for marine biological systems. Among the numerous species impacted, the European lobster (Homarus gammarus) is especially vulnerable to these progressions as it depends on unambiguous ecological circumstances for its endurance and proliferation. In this extensive investigation, we dig into the mind boggling ways environmental change impacts Atlantic waters and, thusly, the living spaces basic for European lobster populaces.

1. **Environmental Change and Maritime Changes in Atlantic Waters:**

   Warming Temperatures:

   The Atlantic Sea isn't invulnerable to the worldwide pattern of climbing temperatures ascribed to environmental change. The warming of Atlantic waters has critical ramifications for marine life, influencing species conveyance, relocation examples, and environment elements. Hotter temperatures influence the metabolic paces of marine creatures, affecting their development, generation, and by and large physiological capabilities.

   Changes in Sea Flows:

   Environmental change modifies sea flows, which assume an essential part in controlling temperature and conveying supplements all through the sea. Changes in these flows can affect the accessibility of prey species for lobsters, influence larval dispersal examples, and impact the network of various marine living spaces. Changes in sea flows may likewise add to the rearrangement of marine species, impacting the arrangement of biological systems.

   Ocean Level Ascent:

   Climbing worldwide temperatures add to the warm extension of seawater and the liquefying of polar ice, prompting ocean level ascent. In Atlantic waters, this ascent presents dangers to waterfront environments, including lobster territories. Expanded flooding, changes in waterfront flows, and modifications to the construction of nearshore conditions can affect the accessibility of appropriate asylum and concealing spots for lobsters.

   Sea Fermentation:

   The retention of overabundance carbon dioxide by the world's seas brings about sea fermentation. While not as articulated in that frame of mind as in a few different districts, fermentation can in any case influence the carbonate science of seawater. This postures dangers to marine creatures with calcium carbonate skeletons, including shell-shaping life forms that are essential for the lobster's territory.

2. **Effect of Environmental Change on Lobster Living spaces:**

Reasonableness of Asylum and Concealing Spots:

Lobsters, including the European lobster, depend on reasonable safe house and concealing spots for assurance from hunters and during shedding processes. Environment actuated changes in ocean level, seaside disintegration, and adjustments to the construction of the sea depths can influence the accessibility and nature of these concealing spots. This, thusly, impacts the weakness of lobsters to predation and their capacity to shed effectively.

Dispersion of Adolescent and Grown-up Lobsters:

The dispersion of lobster populaces is affected by temperature inclinations, prey accessibility, and the design of seaside environments. As temperatures change and prey species shift in light of environmental change, the dispersion of both adolescent and grown-up lobsters might be impacted. Understanding these distributional movements is critical for overseeing lobster fisheries and carrying out preservation measures.

Influence on Regenerative Achievement:

The regenerative outcome of lobsters is unpredictably connected to natural circumstances, including water temperature and the accessibility of appropriate environments for egg-laying. Changes in temperature and natural surroundings quality can impact the timing and progress of proliferation. Understanding these variables is fundamental for anticipating the future overflow of lobster populaces and executing measures to safeguard conceptive living spaces.

Impact on Larval Dispersal:

The dispersal of lobster hatchlings, which happens during the planktonic stage, is affected by sea flows and water temperature. Changes in these natural variables can influence larval dispersal designs, possibly prompting varieties in the network between various lobster territories. Understanding larval dispersal is essential for overseeing and saving lobster populaces despite environmental change.

3. **Environment Driven Difficulties for Lobster Territories:**

Environment Debasement and Waterfront Disintegration:

Environmental change adds to territory debasement through elements, for example, beach front disintegration, storm floods, and ocean level ascent. Lobster living spaces, especially those near the shore, are defenseless against these cycles. Beach front disintegration can lessen the accessibility of reasonable concealing spots for lobsters, affecting their endurance and regenerative achievement.

Changes in Prey Accessibility:

Lobsters are deft omnivores, and their eating routine incorporates an assortment of prey animal groups. Environment prompted changes in sea temperatures and flows can impact the dispersion and overflow of prey species. Changes to the accessibility of prey can influence the taking care of propensities for lobsters, influencing their development rates and by and large wellness.

Outrageous Climate Occasions:

Environmental change is related with an expansion in the recurrence and force of outrageous climate occasions, including tempests and tropical storms. These occasions can make actual harm lobster environments, disturb sea flows, and adjust the design of the sea depths. Lobster populaces might confront expanded death rates and living space debasement because of outrageous climate occasions.

4. **Variations and Reactions of Lobsters to Environmental Change:**

Conduct Transformations:

Lobsters show conduct variations because of changing ecological circumstances. They might change their movement designs, taking care of ways of behaving, and territory use because of temperature varieties. Social pliancy permits lobsters to adapt to momentary changes in their current circumstance.

Physiological Reactions:

Lobsters additionally show physiological reactions to natural changes, remembering varieties for temperature and sea science. These reactions might include changes in metabolic rates, development designs, and regenerative cycles. Understanding the physiological transformations of lobsters is urgent for anticipating their versatility to environmental change.

Relocation and Reach Movements:

Environmental change can drive shifts in the dispersion of lobster populaces as they look for ideal natural circumstances. This might include relocations to more profound waters, toward the north developments to cooler areas, or changes in the profundity inclinations of lobsters. Observing these reach shifts is fundamental for evaluating the effect of environmental change on lobster territories.

Versatile Development:

Throughout longer time scales, lobster populaces might go through versatile development in light of environment driven choice tensions. Hereditary changes that give benefits in hotter or more acidic conditions might turn out to be more pervasive in populaces over ages. Concentrating on the hereditary variety and flexibility of lobster populaces gives bits of knowledge into their drawn out reactions to environmental change.

5. **Protection Techniques for Lobster Territories in an Evolving Environment:**

Territory Security and Rebuilding:

Securing and reestablishing basic lobster living spaces is a foundation of protection systems. Laying out marine safeguarded regions (MPAs), carrying out environment reclamation undertakings, and controlling beach front improvement are crucial parts. These actions give shelters to lobsters, upgrade territory strength, and add to the general maintainability of lobster populaces.

Incorporated Seaside Zone The executives:

Incorporated Waterfront Zone The executives (ICZM) includes an all encompassing way to deal with overseeing beach front regions, taking into account the communications between human exercises and the climate. Executing ICZM rehearses assists balance the requirements of waterfront networks with the preservation of lobster territories. This incorporates practical turn of events, contamination control, and territory preservation.

Environment Tough Fisheries The executives:

Adjusting fisheries the executives practices to the real factors of environmental change is fundamental. This includes changing fishing amounts, carrying out size restricts, and embracing estimates that think about the changing appropriation of lobster populaces. Environment tough fisheries the board guarantees the maintainability of lobster stocks and supports the flexibility of beach front biological systems.

Exploration and Observing Projects:

Putting resources into exploration and observing projects is urgent for understanding the particular effects of environmental change on lobster natural surroundings. This incorporates concentrating on temperature inclinations, prey accessibility, and living space quality for various life phases of lobsters. Long haul observing gives fundamental information to versatile administration techniques.

Local area Commitment and Training:

Connecting with nearby networks in lobster protection endeavors encourages a feeling of shared liability regarding the economical utilization of marine assets. Instructive projects educate the general population about the significance regarding lobster environments, the difficulties they face, and the job people can play in supporting protection endeavors. Local area association adds to the progress of protection drives.

Versatile Administration:

Taking on versatile administration approaches considers adaptability in preservation procedures as new data opens up. This includes routinely rethinking the adequacy of the executives measures, consolidating new logical discoveries, and changing preservation practices to address arising difficulties presented by environmental change.

5.2 Behavioral and physiological adaptations to changing conditions

The capacity of living organic entities to adjust to changing circumstances is a key part of their endurance and developmental achievement. Conduct and physiological transformations assume a critical part in empowering species to adapt to shifts in their current circumstance, whether driven by normal cycles or anthropogenic impacts. In this exhaustive investigation, we dig into the mind boggling components through which life forms display social and physiological variations to evolving conditions. From the minute domain of cell reactions to the mind boggling ways of behaving of higher creatures, this assessment traverses the tremendous variety of life on The planet.

1. **Social Transformations:**

   Characterizing Social Transformations:

   Social transformations envelop the activities, responses, and examples of conduct displayed by creatures in light of changes in their current circumstance. These transformations can upgrade a creature's possibilities of endurance, multiplication, and generally speaking wellness. Social adaptability permits species to take advantage of new open doors, dodge hunters, and explore dynamic environmental scenes.

   Learning and Memory:

   Learning and memory are basic parts of conduct transformations. Organic entities, from straightforward spineless creatures to complex vertebrates, have the ability to gain from encounters and change their way of behaving in like manner. This flexibility is apparent in different settings, like scrounging techniques, hunter aversion, and social communications. The memorable capacity and apply learned data improves a life form's wellness in evolving conditions.

   Regional Way of behaving:

   Regional way of behaving is a typical transformation seen across different taxa. Creatures might lay out and shield regions to get assets, including food, mates, and reasonable settling locales. Territoriality is many times dynamic, with people changing their regional limits in view of variables like asset accessibility, contest, and changing ecological circumstances.

   Movement and Dispersal:

   Relocation and dispersal are boundless social variations that empower species to take advantage of occasional assets, get away from unfriendly circumstances, or colonize new natural surroundings. Birds, well evolved creatures, bugs, and even microorganisms display transient or dispersal ways of behaving. These developments are much of the time set off by ecological signs, like changes in temperature, photoperiod, or asset accessibility.

Correspondence Procedures:

Correspondence is a key social transformation that works with cooperations between people inside an animal categories. Vocalizations, visual presentations, compound signs, and material signals are utilized by living beings to pass on data about domain, mating accessibility, and possible dangers. Versatile changes in correspondence techniques might happen in light of movements in ecological circumstances or to advance flagging productivity.

Social Designs and Collaboration:

Social designs and agreeable ways of behaving are versatile procedures seen in different taxa, including warm blooded creatures, birds, bugs, and social microorganisms. Living in bunches gives advantages like expanded assurance from hunters, proficient scrounging, and agreeable consideration of posterity. Social designs can be dynamic, with people changing their jobs and ways of behaving in view of natural variables.

Circadian Rhythms and Diurnal Examples:

Circadian rhythms, the approximately 24-hour patterns of organic cycles, are unavoidable in the animals of the world collectively. These rhythms, administered by inner organic tickers, impact ways of behaving like taking care of, mating, and rest. Diurnal examples, where exercises are synchronized with sunlight, or nighttime designs, adjusted to evening time conditions, reflect how organic entities advance their conduct because of changing light and temperature cycles.

Hibernation and Lethargy:

Hibernation and lethargy are versatile procedures utilized by specific creatures to moderate energy during times of natural pressure, like winter or food shortage. By entering a condition of diminished metabolic action, these life forms can endure broadened periods without consuming significant assets. The capacity to enter and leave these states is a significant conduct transformation.

Taking care of Methodologies and Dietary Changes:

Changes in asset accessibility, driven by factors like occasional variety or natural surroundings modifications, require changes in taking care of techniques. Social transformations connected with scrounging, prey catch, and food stockpiling add to a creature's capacity to get sustenance in factor conditions. Omnivores, for example, may change their eating routine in view of the wealth of various food sources.

Conceptive Systems:

Conceptive ways of behaving are formed by natural signals, including photoperiod, temperature, and asset accessibility. Species might show transformations like synchronized mating, romance ceremonies, or changes in regenerative timing to augment the probability of effective generation. A few creatures might try and modify their conceptive methodologies in light of populace thickness or social elements.

2. **Physiological Transformations:**

Characterizing Physiological Transformations:

Physiological transformations include changes at the cell, tissue, or organ level that improve a creature's capacity to work in a particular climate. These variations are in many cases driven by specific tensions and add to the general wellness and endurance of an animal groups. Physiological adaptability empowers living beings to flourish in assorted biological specialties.

Temperature Guideline:

Thermoregulation is a key physiological variation that permits creatures to keep an ideal inner temperature. Endothermic (warm-blooded) and ectothermic (unfeeling) creatures utilize various components for temperature guideline. For instance, warm blooded creatures might utilize shuddering or gasping, while reptiles might luxuriate in the sun or look for shade to adjust their internal heat level because of ecological circumstances.

Osmoregulation and Water Equilibrium:

Osmoregulation is the physiological guideline of water and solute focuses inside an organic entity's body. Earthly and sea-going living beings face unmistakable difficulties connected with water balance. Variations, for example, specific excretory designs, social changes in water-chasing or aversion, and effective filtration systems add to osmoregulatory abilities.

Breath and Gas Trade:

Effective gas trade is significant for organic entities to gain oxygen and oust carbon dioxide. Transformations in respiratory designs, like gills, lungs, or tracheal frameworks, improve gas trade in view of natural circumstances. Sea-going living beings, for example, may have gills for extricating oxygen from water, while earthbound creatures might depend on lungs for air relaxing.

Metabolic Pathway Changes:

Changes in natural circumstances, like food accessibility or temperature, can provoke changes in metabolic pathways. Organic entities might move among high-impact and anaerobic digestion, change energy capacity methodologies, or change metabolic rates to match ecological requests. These physiological variations improve energy use and add to generally speaking metabolic proficiency.

Sub-atomic Reactions to Stress:

At the sub-atomic level, living beings display reactions to stressors through systems, for example, the actuation of stress proteins, DNA fix cycles, and changes in quality articulation. These sub-atomic variations add to the organic entity's capacity to endure natural pressure, including factors like outrageous temperatures, contaminations, or vacillations in supplement accessibility.

Lethargy and Calmness:

Lethargy and peacefulness are physiological variations that permit organic entities to enter conditions of decreased movement and digestion during ominous circumstances. Seeds might enter lethargy to endure times of dry spell, while creatures might enter quiet to preserve energy during seasons of food shortage. These states empower creatures to persevere through testing conditions until additional great conditions emerge.

Insusceptible Framework Reactions:

The safe framework assumes a critical part in protecting organic entities against microorganisms and keeping up with generally wellbeing. Physiological transformations in the resistant framework consider reactions to changing pathogenic difficulties. These transformations might remember varieties for invulnerable cell movement, immune response creation, and the acknowledgment of explicit microbes in view of ecological openness.

Resilience to Outrageous Conditions:

A few creatures flourish in outrageous conditions, like high temperatures, acidic circumstances, or high saltiness. Physiological variations, including specific chemicals, film structures, and metabolic pathways, empower these extremophiles to endure conditions that would be adverse to different species. Models incorporate thermophilic microorganisms in underground aquifers or halophiles in saline conditions.

Conceptive Physiology:

Regenerative physiology includes variations connected with the conceptive cycles of a living being. Natural prompts, like temperature or photoperiod, may impact regenerative chemical delivery and gamete advancement. Physiological transformations in regenerative organs, mating ways of behaving, and preparation techniques add to the conceptive progress of an animal categories.

3. **Intuitive Variations:**

Conduct Physiology Connections:

The exchange among social and physiological variations is clear in numerous organic entities. For instance, a creature's reaction to a changing climate might include both conduct changes, for example, looking for shade or modifying action designs, and physiological changes, for example, expanding metabolic rates or changing water balance. These intuitive transformations upgrade an organic entity's general capacity to adapt to ecological difficulties.

Compromises and Energy Distribution:

Organic entities frequently face compromises while allotting assets to various parts of their science, like development, multiplication, and safeguard. Conduct and physiological transformations mirror the difficult exercise between these contending needs. For example, a creature might distribute energy to improved insusceptible capability during times of uplifted pathogenic gamble, regardless of whether it comes to the detriment of other physiological cycles.

Transformative Points of view:

Conduct and physiological variations have significant ramifications for the developmental directions of species. Normal choice follows up on varieties in conduct and physiology, inclining toward qualities that improve a living's ability to be to make due and imitate. After some time, these variations become imbued in a populace's hereditary cosmetics, impacting its ability to flourish in unambiguous natural specialties.

Phenotypic Pliancy:

Phenotypic pliancy alludes to the capacity of a living being to communicate various aggregates in light of differing natural circumstances. Social and physiological transformations might display phenotypic versatility, permitting people to change their characteristics in view of natural signs. This adaptability adds to the flexibility of species notwithstanding evolving conditions.

4. **Contextual analyses Across Taxa:**

Icy and Antarctic Variations:

Creatures occupying polar districts face outrageous ecological circumstances, including low temperatures, broadened times of dimness, and moving admittance to assets. Conduct and physiological variations in Icy and Antarctic species, like polar bears, penguins, and extremophiles, feature the particular systems that empower endurance in these brutal conditions.

Desert Transformations:

Desert biological systems present interesting difficulties, described by high temperatures, low water accessibility, and parched conditions. Organic entities like camels, prickly plants, and desert-staying bugs grandstand social and physiological variations that boost water protection, direct internal heat level, and improve asset use in desert conditions.

Oceanic Transformations:

Oceanic conditions, including freshwater and marine natural surroundings, present assorted difficulties for creatures. From the remote ocean transformations of anglerfish to the movement examples of salmon, sea-going species exhibit a large number of social and physiological variations that empower them to flourish in various water conditions.

Chapter 6

Research Methods And Techniques

Research is the foundation of logical request, adding to the extension of information, the advancement of new innovations, and the comprehension of perplexing peculiarities. The strategies and procedures utilized in research are different, going from trial plans in labs to observational examinations in regular habitats. In this investigation, we dive into the rich woven artwork of examination strategies and procedures, analyzing their subtleties, applications, and commitments to the headway of different fields.

1. **Prologue to Exploration Techniques:**
   Definition and Reason:
   Research strategies allude to the efficient cycles and methods utilized to assemble, investigate, and decipher information to address research questions or testing speculations. The all-encompassing objective is to gain solid and substantial data that adds to the comprehension of peculiarities, the advancement of hypotheses, or the improvement of functional applications.
   Kinds of Exploration:
   Examination can be comprehensively ordered into subjective and quantitative methodologies. Subjective exploration centers around figuring out the hidden implications, inspirations, and settings of peculiarities through strategies, for example, interviews, contextual investigations, and content examination. Quantitative examination, then again, underscores mathematical information and measurable investigation, utilizing techniques like tests, overviews, and observational examinations.

2. **Quantitative Exploration Strategies:**
   Exploratory Exploration:
   Exploratory examination includes controlling free factors to notice their

consequences for subordinate factors while controlling for puzzling elements. This technique, frequently directed in lab settings, permits analysts to lay out causal connections. Randomized controlled preliminaries (RCTs) are a typical type of trial research utilized in fields like medication and brain science.

Overview Exploration:

Overviews are broadly utilized to gather information from countless members. Polls or meetings are utilized to accumulate data on perspectives, ways of behaving, feelings, and segment attributes. Overview research is significant for concentrating on friendly patterns, general suppositions, and examples inside populaces.

Observational Exploration:

Observational exploration includes efficiently watching and recording ways of behaving, occasions, or peculiarities without impedance. This strategy is normally utilized in fields like human sciences, brain research, and nature. Naturalistic perception happens in true settings, while organized perception includes predefined rules for information assortment.

Correlational Exploration:

Correlational exploration investigates the connections between factors without controlling them. Measurable examinations, like connection coefficients, are utilized to decide the strength and bearing of affiliations. Correlational examinations add to distinguishing designs and foreseeing results however don't lay out causation.

Longitudinal and Cross-Sectional Investigations:

Longitudinal investigations track similar members over a drawn out period to look at changes and patterns over the long run. Cross-sectional examinations, conversely, gather information from members at a solitary moment. The two methodologies give significant experiences into formative examples, patterns, and connections.

Meta-Examination:

Meta-examination includes consolidating and investigating information from various investigations to reach more vigorous determinations. This technique permits analysts to orchestrate discoveries from different sources, expanding factual power and generalizability. Meta-examinations are normal in medication, brain research, and sociologies.

3. **Subjective Exploration Strategies:**

Interviews:

Interviews in subjective exploration include connecting with members in unassuming discussions to investigate their viewpoints, encounters, and implications ascribed to peculiarities. Organized, semi-organized, or unstructured meetings give adaptability to inside and out investigation.

Center Gatherings:

Center gatherings unite a little, different gathering of members to examine a particular subject under the direction of a mediator. This strategy encourages collective vibes and creates rich subjective information by catching different points of view and associations.

Contextual investigations:

Contextual investigations include a top to bottom examination of a solitary individual, gathering, occasion, or peculiarity. Scientists gather and dissect various sorts of information, including meetings, archives, and perceptions. Contextual investigations are significant for investigating complex, setting subordinate peculiarities.

Content Investigation:

Content investigation is a deliberate way to deal with breaking down literary, visual, or sound substance to distinguish examples, subjects, and implications. This technique is frequently used to break down media content, reports, or correspondence antiques.

Grounded Hypothesis:

Grounded hypothesis is an iterative and efficient way to deal with creating speculations from subjective information. Analysts start with open coding, recognizing topics and examples, and continuously refine the hypothesis through consistent correlation and hypothetical inspecting.

Ethnography:

Ethnography includes submerging specialists in the way of life or local area being examined. Through member perception and top to bottom meetings, ethnographers gain an all encompassing comprehension of social practices, convictions, and collaborations inside a particular setting.

4. **Blended Techniques Exploration:**

Definition and Reconciliation:

Blended techniques research joins both quantitative and subjective methodologies inside a solitary report. This approach means to use the qualities of the two strategies, giving a more far reaching comprehension of examination questions. Coordination can happen at various stages, including information assortment, investigation, and understanding.

Consecutive and Simultaneous Plans:

In consecutive plans, specialists first gather and dissect information utilizing one strategy prior to utilizing the other technique in a resulting stage. Simultaneous plans include gathering and breaking down the two kinds of information all the while. Blended strategies research takes into account triangulation, improving the legitimacy and dependability of discoveries.

5. **Information Assortment Methods:**

Overviews and Polls:

Overviews and polls are apparatuses for gathering self-report information from members. Cautious plan, including clear and fair inquiries, guarantees the dependability and legitimacy of reactions. Online reviews have become progressively famous for their availability and cost-viability.

Interviews:

Interviews, whether organized, semi-organized, or unstructured, permit analysts to accumulate inside and out data straightforwardly from members. Questioners should lay out compatibility, pose unassuming inquiries, and effectively pay attention to get significant reactions.

Perception:

Observational strategies include deliberately watching and recording ways of behaving, occasions, or peculiarities. Analysts should foster clear conventions, limit spectator predisposition, and address moral contemplations while utilizing observational techniques.

Tests:

Tests include controlling autonomous factors to notice their impacts on subordinate factors. Trial plans require randomization, control gatherings, and cautious estimation to guarantee interior legitimacy.

Hands on work:

Hands on work includes leading examination in normal settings, permitting scientists to notice and communicate with members straightforwardly. Ethnographic hands on work, for instance, requires delayed commitment to catch the subtleties of social and social settings.

Chronicled Exploration:

Chronicled research includes breaking down existing records, archives, or relics to respond to explore questions. This approach is significant for verifiable examinations, content examination, and examinations that depend on prior information.

6. **Information Examination Procedures:**

Measurable Investigation:

Measurable examination is central to quantitative exploration, including the use of factual tests to decide connections, contrasts, or examples in mathematical information. Normal factual tests incorporate t-tests, ANOVA, relapse investigation, and chi-square tests.

Subjective Coding:

Subjective coding includes sorting and marking information to distinguish topics, examples, or implications. Open coding, pivotal coding, and particular coding are steps in the coding system that help sort out and figure out subjective information.

Topical Investigation:

Topical investigation is a strategy for distinguishing, dissecting, and revealing examples (subjects) inside subjective information. Specialists methodicallly arrange and decipher information to produce experiences into the exploration questions.

Content Examination:

Content examination includes deliberately dissecting literary, visual, or sound substance to distinguish examples, subjects, and implications. Coding classifications are created to arrange and decipher content in light of predefined standards.

Grounded Hypothesis Coding:

Grounded hypothesis coding follows an iterative course of open coding, hub coding, and specific coding to foster speculations grounded in subjective information. This technique permits analysts to infer ideas and classifications straightforwardly from the information.

7. **Moral Contemplations in Exploration:**

Informed Assent:

Informed assent is a foundation of moral exploration, guaranteeing that members are completely mindful of the review's motivation, methods, dangers, and advantages prior to consenting to take an interest. Specialists should give clear and fathomable data and regard members' independence.

Secrecy and Namelessness:

Safeguarding members' secrecy and namelessness is fundamental. Analysts should go to lengths to shield members' characters and guarantee that delicate data isn't revealed without assent.

Research Honesty:

Research trustworthiness includes keeping up with genuineness and straightforwardness in all phases of the exploration cycle. Scientists should report discoveries precisely, unveil irreconcilable circumstances, and stick to moral principles laid out by proficient associations and organizations.

Limiting Damage:

Scientists are committed to limit damage to members, both physical and mental. This incorporates keeping away from superfluous dangers, giving suitable post-op interview, and offering support administrations assuming members experience trouble.

Consideration and Variety:

Moral exploration rehearses include advancing inclusivity and variety. Analysts should guarantee that their investigations think about the points of view of different populaces and abstain from supporting generalizations or sustaining imbalances.

8. **Propels in Exploration Strategies:**

Innovative Progressions:

Innovation has reformed research strategies, giving new instruments and methods to information assortment and examination. The utilization of wearable gadgets, versatile applications, computer generated reality, and man-made reasoning has extended the opportunities for concentrating on human way of behaving, well-being, and comprehension.

Enormous Information and Information Science:

The approach of huge information has changed research by empowering the examination of enormous, complex datasets. Information science procedures, including AI and information mining, permit specialists to get significant experiences from immense measures of data in fields like hereditary qualities, financial aspects, and sociologies.

Interdisciplinary Methodologies:

Interdisciplinary exploration approaches include cooperation across various scholarly disciplines. Incorporating different viewpoints and techniques can prompt more exhaustive and nuanced understandings of perplexing issues, cultivating advancement and critical thinking.

Local area Based Exploration:

Local area based research includes coordinated effort among analysts and local area individuals to resolve neighborhood issues. This approach perceives the skill and information inside networks, underscoring participatory strategies and guaranteeing that exploration helps the local area.

6.1 Overview of methodologies used in studying European Lobster

The investigation of the European lobster (Homarus gammarus) incorporates a different exhibit of techniques intended to unwind the intricacies of its science, nature, conduct, and protection. As a cornerstone animal groups in marine environments, the European lobster assumes a significant part in keeping up with biological equilibrium, and grasping its life history, dissemination, and conduct is fundamental for powerful administration and preservation. This complete outline investigates the strategies utilized in concentrating on European lobsters, digging into research moves toward that length lab examinations to handle studies and featuring the interdisciplinary idea of lobster research.

1. **Life History and Conceptive Science:**
   Research center Trials:
   Research center trials are principal for concentrating on the existence history and conceptive science of European lobsters. Controlled conditions permit analysts to control factors like temperature, saltiness, and photoperiod to notice lobster conduct, development, and regenerative cycles.
   Shed Cycle Perceptions:
   Noticing the shed cycle is urgent for figuring out the development and regenerative phases of lobsters. Specialists lead shed cycle perceptions in

imprisonment, noticing shedding recurrence, changes in exoskeleton hardness, and related ways of behaving.

Histological Methods:

Histological methods include inspecting lobster tissues at a minuscule level to concentrate on conceptive organs. This approach gives experiences into gonadal turn of events, development, and regenerative cycles. Taken apart tissues are handled, segmented, and stained for infinitesimal examination.

Labeling and Imprint Recover Studies:

Labeling and mark-recover concentrates on in the wild add to understanding lobster relocation designs, populace elements, and life span. Lobsters are labeled with remarkably coded labels, and ensuing recovers give information on development rates, developments, and populace size.

Hereditary Examinations:

Hereditary examinations, including DNA sequencing and microsatellite markers, offer experiences into the hereditary variety, relatedness, and populace construction of European lobster populaces. Atomic procedures add to fisheries the executives and protection endeavors.

2. **Biology and Dissemination:**

Field Overviews:

Field overviews include the precise assortment of information on lobster circulation and overflow in their regular environments. Jumpers, remotely worked vehicles (ROVs), or traps are utilized to review various profundities, substrates, and districts.

Bedeviled Far off Submerged Video (BRUV):

BRUV frameworks are conveyed on the ocean bottom with trap to draw in lobsters. Video film catches lobster presence, overflow, and conduct. This non-meddlesome technique is significant for concentrating on lobsters right at home.

Submerged Perceptions:

Direct perceptions by jumpers give significant subjective information on lobster conduct, collaborations, and environment use. Submerged investigations are fundamental for archiving parts of lobster environment that might be trying to catch utilizing different techniques.

Telemetry:

Telemetry includes joining electronic labels to lobsters to follow their developments. Acoustic or satellite labels give constant or recorded information on lobster movement designs, living space inclinations, and reactions to ecological changes.

GIS and Spatial Examinations:

Geographic Data Framework (GIS) apparatuses and spatial examinations help in figuring out the spatial conveyance of lobster populaces. Planning territory inclinations, movement courses, and spatial connections add to compelling marine spatial preparation.

3. **Social Environment:**

Research facility Perceptions:

Research facility perceptions take into account controlled probes lobster conduct. Specialists concentrate on reactions to boosts, taking care of propensities, and social communications in a controlled setting, giving bits of knowledge into individual and gathering ways of behaving.

Field Investigations:

Field tests include controlling ecological factors to concentrate on lobster conduct right at home. This might incorporate exploring the effect of predation chance, contest, or natural surroundings structure on lobster conduct.

Acoustic Observing:

Acoustic observing uses submerged mouthpieces (hydrophones) to record sounds delivered by lobsters. Acoustic prompts assume a part in lobster correspondence, mating, and route. Acoustic checking adds to grasping their acoustic environment.

Respirometry:

Respirometry estimates oxygen utilization to survey the metabolic rates and energy use of lobsters. This strategy helps with grasping how ecological elements, like temperature or toxins, impact lobster physiology and conduct.

Electrophysiological Studies:

Electrophysiological studies include recording the electrical movement of lobster nerves or tactile organs. This approach gives bits of knowledge into lobster tangible insight, including reactions to substance signs, light, and contact.

4. **Fisheries The board:**

Trap Overviews:

Trap overviews include sending lobster traps in unambiguous regions to survey get rates, size circulation, and populace elements. Observing snare gets over the long run adds to surveying the soundness of lobster fisheries.

Natural Testing:

Natural testing includes gathering information on lobster size, sex, and regenerative status from caught people. This data is vital for laying out size limits, evaluating populace structure, and deciding fishing seasons.

Stock Appraisals:

Stock appraisals join information from different sources, including trap overviews, tag-recover studies, and organic inspecting, to assess populace size, development rates, and fishing mortality. This data guides feasible fisheries the executives.

Financial Reviews:

Financial studies evaluate the monetary worth of lobster fisheries. Scientists concentrate on market patterns, shopper inclinations, and the monetary effect of lobster fishing on nearby networks.

Demonstrating Approaches:

Numerical models, for example, populace elements models and bioeconomic models, help in anticipating the effect of various administration systems on lobster populaces and fisheries manageability. These models consider factors like enlistment, mortality, and fishing exertion.

5. **Protection and Natural Observing:**

Ecological DNA (eDNA) Testing:

eDNA inspecting includes gathering hereditary material shed by living beings into the climate. This harmless strategy gives data on the presence of species, including intriguing or tricky lobsters, and is important for ecological observing.

Environment Appraisals:

Surveying lobster living spaces includes concentrating on the attributes of ocean bottom substrates, temperature systems, and water quality in regions visited by lobsters. Understanding territory inclinations adds to preservation endeavors.

Environmental Change Studies:

Environmental change concentrates on center around surveying the effect of environment related factors, for example, temperature increase and sea fermentation, on lobster populaces. This interdisciplinary exploration joins environmental and physiological methodologies.

Local area Commitment and Resident Science:

Local area commitment and resident science include cooperation with neighborhood networks and non-researchers in information assortment. This approach encourages a feeling of stewardship and integrates customary environmental information into preservation drives.

Remote Detecting:

Remote detecting advances, including satellite symbolism and elevated reviews, give significant information for enormous scope natural changes. Checking ocean surface temperature, sea flows, and living space adjustments helps with anticipating the impacts of environmental change on lobster biological systems.

6. **Progresses in Lobster Exploration Philosophies:**

Genomic and Transcriptomic Examinations:

Progresses in genomics and transcriptomics have opened new roads for concentrating on the sub-atomic components hidden lobster science. Sequencing the lobster genome and investigating quality articulation profiles improve how we might interpret transformation and development.

Biotelemetry and Information Logging:

Biotelemetry and information logging innovations have become more refined, empowering scientists to gather continuous information on lobster conduct, physiology, and natural associations. This innovation improves the accuracy and goal of natural investigations.

AI and Information Investigation:

AI calculations and information investigation add to the examination of complex datasets, distinguishing examples, and making forecasts. These methodologies are progressively applied in examinations including huge scope observing, like acoustic telemetry information.

3D Imaging and Displaying:

3D imaging advancements, including submerged photogrammetry and laser checking, permit scientists to make definite models of lobster territories and individual lobsters. These models help in environment evaluations and concentrating on lobster morphology.

6.2 Technological advancements in lobster research

Innovative progressions have changed the scene of marine examination, empowering researchers to investigate the perplexing existences of marine creatures with phenomenal accuracy and profundity. On account of lobster research, imaginative innovations play had a significant impact in unwinding the secrets of these notable scavangers. This complete investigation dives into the range of mechanical progressions that have pushed lobster research forward, covering regions from following and observing to hereditary examinations and submerged imaging.

1. **Following and Observing Advances:**

   Telemetry and Acoustic Following:

   Telemetry has upset the investigation of lobster conduct and developments. Acoustic labels joined to lobsters radiate signs that are recognized by submerged recipients, permitting analysts to follow individual lobsters in their normal living spaces. This innovation gives bits of knowledge into relocation designs, living space inclinations, and reactions to ecological changes.

   Satellite Following:

   Satellite following expands the scope of lobster examination to tremendous maritime fields. Lobsters furnished with satellite labels send information on their areas, permitting analysts to screen significant distance developments and maritime movements. This innovation has suggestions for grasping populace network and overseeing transboundary lobster stocks.

Information Logging and Biotelemetry:

Information logging gadgets and biotelemetry frameworks have become progressively modern, giving constant data on lobster conduct, physiology, and ecological collaborations. These gadgets are intended to be negligibly obtrusive, offering important bits of knowledge into viewpoints like taking care of examples, temperature inclinations, and reactions to anthropogenic aggravations.

Remote Detecting and Ethereal Reviews:

Remote detecting innovations, including satellite symbolism and ethereal studies, add to the checking of lobster territories for an enormous scope. These devices offer experiences into natural factors, for example, ocean surface temperature, water lucidity, and ocean bottom attributes. Flying reviews give a 10,000 foot perspective of beach front regions, supporting environment evaluations and stock checking.

2. **Hereditary and Atomic Advances:**

Genomic Sequencing:

The sequencing of the lobster genome has been a milestone accomplishment in lobster research. Genomic data gives an outline to figuring out the sub-atomic systems fundamental lobster science, development, and transformation. It opens roads for concentrating on hereditary variety, recognizing key qualities, and disentangling the genomic premise of characteristics applicable to protection and fisheries the executives.

Atomic Markers and Microsatellites:

Atomic markers, including microsatellites, are utilized in hereditary examinations to evaluate populace construction, relatedness, and hereditary variety. These markers help in separating populaces, distinguishing source-sink elements, and adding to viable preservation procedures. Microsatellite information assume a critical part in stock evaluations and grasping the hereditary premise of versatile characteristics.

Ecological DNA (eDNA) Examining:

eDNA inspecting addresses a painless way to deal with concentrating on lobster populaces. Ecological DNA shed by lobsters into their environmental factors can be gathered and examined to distinguish the presence of the species. This procedure is especially significant for observing interesting or subtle lobster populaces and evaluating living space reasonableness.

Transcriptomics and Quality Articulation Profiling:

Transcriptomic examinations include concentrating on the statement of qualities in unambiguous tissues or under various circumstances. This approach gives bits of knowledge into how lobsters answer natural stressors, micro-organisms, or changes in their environments. Quality articulation profiling adds to figuring out the sub-atomic premise of lobster physiology and conduct.

3. **Imaging and Representation Advancements:**

Submerged Photogrammetry:

Submerged photogrammetry includes catching a progression of photos of submerged conditions and utilizing programming to recreate three-layered (3D) models. This innovation is applied to concentrate on lobster environments, ocean bottom geology, and the morphology of individual lobsters. The subsequent 3D models offer point by point bits of knowledge into submerged environments.

Laser Checking and LiDAR:

Laser checking innovations, including Light Recognition and Running (LiDAR), empower exact planning of submerged structures. LiDAR can infiltrate water to catch point by point geological information, giving high-goal pictures of lobster natural surroundings. These advancements are instrumental in living space evaluations and investigations of beach front geomorphology.

ROVs and AUVs:

Remotely Worked Vehicles (ROVs) and Independent Submerged Vehicles (AUVs) are imperative instruments for investigating the remote ocean domains where lobsters live. Outfitted with cameras and sensors, these mechanical vehicles permit specialists to direct definite reviews, notice lobster conduct, and gather ecological information at critical profundities.

Teased Distant Submerged Video (BRUV):

BRUV frameworks are intended to draw in marine life to a bedeviled camera arrangement. This innovation is especially valuable for concentrating on lobster populaces, conduct, and communications in their regular environments. BRUV gives non-meddling perceptions, catching a preview of the marine climate and its occupants.

4. **AI and Information Examination:**

Standard of conduct Acknowledgment:

AI calculations are utilized to perceive and break down standards of conduct showed by lobsters. This incorporates the recognizable proof of explicit developments, taking care of ways of behaving, and reactions to natural improvements. Personal conduct standard acknowledgment improves the productivity of information investigation and considers the mechanized handling of huge datasets.

Populace Displaying:

AI and information investigation add to the advancement of populace models that reproduce the elements of lobster populaces. These models coordinate natural factors, fishing exertion, and organic boundaries to foresee populace patterns, enlistment designs, and the effect of various administration methodologies.

Enormous Information Investigation:

The coming of large information investigation has changed the manner in which scientists process and decipher immense datasets. In lobster research, huge information examination empower the extraction of significant experiences from different sources, including telemetry information, hereditary data, and natural factors. This comprehensive methodology improves how we might interpret the intricate connections molding lobster environments.

5. **Challenges and Moral Contemplations:**

Security and Moral Utilization of Innovation:

As innovation propels, there is a need to address protection concerns and moral contemplations related with following and observing advancements. Finding some kind of harmony between logical investigation and the moral treatment of marine life forms is critical to guarantee dependable and practical lobster research.

Information Security and The board:

The rising dependence on innovation for information assortment and examination requires hearty information safety efforts. Scientists should execute conventions to shield delicate data, particularly in examinations including hereditary information or the areas of touchy lobster environments.

Interdisciplinary Cooperation:

The coordination of different advancements in lobster research requires interdisciplinary joint effort. Researchers, engineers, information researchers, and ethicists should cooperate to bridle the maximum capacity of innovative progressions while tending to the moral ramifications and restrictions of every technique.

6. **Future Headings and Suggestions:**

Accuracy Protection and The executives:

Innovative headways empower accuracy protection and the executives methodologies for lobster populaces. The capacity to screen individual lobsters, evaluate hereditary variety, and foresee populace patterns adds to more powerful and designated protection endeavors.

Environmental Change Flexibility:

Even with environmental change, innovative instruments offer chances to concentrate on how lobsters answer ecological movements. Understanding their versatile limit and possible effects on dissemination and conduct gives important data to environment strong administration techniques.

Schooling and Effort:

Mechanical developments in lobster research present open doors for training and effort. Connecting with the general population through computer generated simulation encounters, live gushing of submerged reviews, or resident science drives cultivates a more noteworthy comprehension of marine environments and the significance of lobster preservation.

Advancement in Maintainable Hydroponics:

Mechanical headways assume a part in the maintainable improvement of lobster hydroponics. Further developed observing of hydroponics conditions, accuracy taking care of in light of conduct information, and hereditary choice for helpful qualities add to the capable extension of lobster cultivating.

6.3 Challenges and future prospects in lobster research

The domain of lobster research, regardless of huge headways, isn't without its difficulties. From the intricacies of economical fisheries the executives to the complicated elements of lobster biology, analysts face leaps that require creative arrangements. This investigation dives into the key difficulties right now looked by lobster analysts and layouts the promising future possibilities that could shape the direction of lobster research in the years to come.

1. **Challenges in Lobster Exploration:**

    Overexploitation and Fisheries The board:

    Lobster populaces overall are vulnerable to overexploitation because of popularity in the fish business. Finding some kind of harmony between satisfying business sector needs and guaranteeing the supportability of lobster fisheries is a considerable test. The adequacy of existing fisheries the executives techniques, including size cutoff points, standards, and occasional terminations, is much of the time impeded by unlawful fishing and lacking requirement.

    Environmental Change Effect:

    Lobster populaces are delicate to ecological changes, and environmental change represents a critical danger. Increasing ocean temperatures, sea fermentation, and adjusted sea flows can influence the appropriation, proliferation, and in general strength of lobsters. Understanding what these progressions mean for lobster living spaces and populaces is urgent for creating versatile administration procedures.

    Natural surroundings Corruption and Misfortune:

    Human exercises, like base fishing and seaside improvement, add to natural surroundings debasement and misfortune for lobsters. Disastrous fishing practices can harm basic living spaces like seagrass beds and rough reefs. Recognizing and relieving the effects of environment corruption are fundamental for the drawn out wellbeing of lobster populaces.

    Illness and Microbes:

    Lobsters are defenseless to different infections, and flare-ups can have extreme ramifications for populaces. The spread of microorganisms, for example, the lobster shell illness brought about by microbes, represents a test to both wild and hydroponics populaces. Examination into sickness anticipation, recognition, and the executives is critical for keeping up with solid lobster populaces.

Hereditary Variety and Transformation:

Keeping up with hereditary variety is fundamental for the flexibility and versatility of lobster populaces. Overharvesting, living space discontinuity, and environmental change can diminish hereditary variety, restricting the capacity of lobsters to adjust to changing natural circumstances. Grasping the hereditary premise of attributes and advancing hereditary variety are basic for the drawn out endurance of lobster populaces.

Associations with Obtrusive Species:

Lobster natural surroundings might be impacted by the presentation of obtrusive species, either straightforwardly or through changes in biological system elements. Obtrusive species can rival lobsters for assets, modify food networks, and present new infections. Contemplating and relieving the effects of intrusive species is fundamental for protecting the equilibrium of marine environments.

Innovative and Monetary Requirements:

While innovative progressions offer important instruments for lobster research, there are difficulties connected with access and reasonableness. Not all specialists or districts might have the assets to convey refined advances like telemetry, hereditary sequencing, or submerged imaging. Connecting these mechanical holes is fundamental for guaranteeing far reaching and fair lobster research.

2. **Future Possibilities in Lobster Exploration:**

Headways in Reasonable Fisheries The board:

Future possibilities in lobster research include refining and growing economical fisheries the board rehearses. This incorporates the advancement of cutting edge checking frameworks, further developed consistence measures, and the mix of information driven approaches. Embracing innovation, for example, constant following and information examination, can improve the accuracy and viability of fisheries the executives.

Environment Tough Lobster Populaces:

Adjusting lobster populaces to environmental change is a critical concentration for future exploration. Understanding the hereditary premise of temperature resistance and other versatile characteristics can illuminate particular reproducing programs that advance environment flexibility. Moreover, checking and displaying the effects of environmental change on lobster living spaces will add to the improvement of proactive protection techniques.

Natural surroundings Reclamation and Assurance:

Future endeavors in lobster examination ought to focus on natural surroundings rebuilding and security drives. Cooperative undertakings that draw in neighborhood networks, researchers, and policymakers can make progress toward saving basic lobster territories. Distinguishing and assigning marine safeguarded regions can offer places of refuge for lobsters to flourish and add to by and large marine biodiversity.

Infection The executives and Biosecurity:

Examination into lobster illness the board and biosecurity estimates will be significant for the reasonable improvement of both wild and hydroponics populaces. This incorporates the advancement of illness safe lobster strains, early identification techniques, and the execution of biosecurity conventions to forestall the spread of microbes.

Imaginative Hydroponics Practices:

The fate of lobster research remembers advancements for hydroponics practices to fulfill expanding market need economically. This includes upgrading incubation center methods, working on larval raising circumstances, and creating advancements for coastal lobster hydroponics. Incorporating hydroponics with biological standards can limit natural effects.

Resident Science and Local area Commitment:

Drawing in people in general through resident science drives can contribute important information to lobster research. Nearby people group, anglers, and sporting jumpers can become accomplices in information assortment, environment observing, and preservation endeavors. This cooperative methodology cultivates a feeling of stewardship and fortifies the association among examination and local area interests.

Trend setting innovations for Checking and Observation:

Proceeded with headways in innovation will assume a vital part in improving checking and reconnaissance capacities. Scaled down sensors, high level imaging advances, and AI applications can give constant information on lobster conduct, populace elements, and natural circumstances. These advances empower more productive and financially savvy information assortment.

Global Coordinated effort and Information Sharing:

Tending to worldwide difficulties in lobster research requires global joint effort and information sharing. Laying out networks for data trade, cooperative exploration ventures, and joint protection drives can encourage an aggregate comprehension of lobster populaces and advance prescribed procedures in fisheries the board.

Public Mindfulness and Instruction:

Future possibilities in lobster research include raising public mindfulness and advancing training about the significance of lobster protection. Outreach programs, instructive materials, and intuitive displays can engage networks to add to the assurance of lobster natural surroundings and backing reasonable fishing rehearses.

3. **Coordinated Approaches and Interdisciplinary Exploration:**

All encompassing Environment The executives:

Future lobster exploration ought to take on all encompassing environment the executives draws near. Understanding the interconnectedness of lobster populaces with other marine species and environment elements is significant. Coordinated administration techniques that consider the more extensive biological setting will add to the strength of lobster environments.

Interdisciplinary Joint effort:

Cooperative endeavors between researchers from different disciplines, including science, hereditary qualities, oceanography, and sociologies, are fundamental for thorough lobster research. Interdisciplinary coordinated effort empowers specialists to address complex difficulties, think about different viewpoints, and foster all encompassing arrangements that benefit both lobster populaces and the networks that rely upon them.

Moral Contemplations in Exploration:

The fate of lobster research includes a guarantee to moral contemplations. Scientists should focus on the government assistance of lobster populaces, limit hurt during information assortment, and participate in straightforward and capable practices. Moral rules ought to develop close by innovative headways to guarantee the moral utilization of arising advancements.

Chapter 7

Aquaculture Potential And Conclusion

The idea of hydroponics, or the controlled development of sea-going creatures, has acquired noticeable quality as a suitable answer for address the difficulties looked by wild lobster populaces. While by and large, the lobster business has essentially depended on wild collects, the rising interest for lobster and worries about overfishing have prompted a developing interest in hydroponics as a correlative or elective source. Investigating the hydroponics potential for lobsters includes contemplations going from incubation facility practices to coastal cultivating advancements.

Incubator Methods:

Hydroponics of lobsters frequently starts with incubator activities where hatchlings are refined in controlled conditions. Creating effective and solid incubation center strategies is pivotal for guaranteeing a reliable stock of adolescent lobsters. This includes advancing water quality, nourishment, and temperature conditions to help larval development and improvement.

Larval Raising:

Larval raising is a basic stage in lobster hydroponics, as it includes supporting the little hatchlings into adolescent stages. Giving proper nourishment, observing ecological circumstances, and overseeing larval densities are fundamental parts of fruitful larval raising. Progresses in larval sustenance, including the advancement of specific feeds, add to the general outcome of hydroponics activities.

Adolescent Creation:

Progressing hatchlings into adolescent stages requires cautious regard for ecological circumstances and the arrangement of appropriate territories. Adolescent lobsters are many times kept in tanks or raceways that mirror normal circumstances. Checking development rates, improving taking care of practices, and guaranteeing suitable asylum and substrate are fundamental parts of adolescent lobster creation.

Coastal Hydroponics Frameworks:

Coastal hydroponics frameworks have acquired ubiquity as a maintainable and harmless to the ecosystem way to deal with lobster cultivating. These frameworks include the development of lobsters in land-based offices, giving better command over water quality, temperature, and sickness the executives. Coastal hydroponics limits the natural effect related with conventional vast water cultivating.

Recycling Hydroponics Frameworks (RAS):

Recycling Hydroponics Frameworks (RAS) are a kind of inland framework that constantly channels and reuses water. RAS innovation guarantees proficient utilization of water assets, lessens the gamble of sickness transmission, and takes into account all year lobster creation. Executing RAS in lobster hydroponics improves supportability and limits the natural impression of cultivating activities.

Supportable Taking care of Practices:

Supportable taking care of practices are basic to capable lobster hydroponics. Specialists and aquaculturists investigate elective feeds that decrease dependence on wild-gotten fish as an essential protein source. Growing healthfully adjusted and harmless to the ecosystem takes care of adds to the general manageability of lobster cultivating.

II. Challenges in Lobster Hydroponics:

While the potential for lobster hydroponics is promising, it isn't without challenges. Addressing these difficulties is fundamental to guarantee the achievement and manageability of hydroponics tasks:

Sickness The executives:

Illness flare-ups can represent a huge danger to lobster hydroponics. Nearness in hydroponics frameworks expands the gamble of illness transmission. Creating viable sickness avoidance and the board techniques, including biosecurity measures, is significant for the outcome of lobster hydroponics.

Hereditary Variety and Specific Reproducing:

Keeping up with hereditary variety is a test in hydroponics settings where populaces might be restricted. Inbreeding can prompt decreased flexibility and versatility. Carrying out particular reproducing programs that focus on hereditary variety and positive attributes is fundamental for the drawn out progress of hydroponics tasks.

Ecological Effect:

While inland hydroponics frameworks mean to limit natural effect, worries about supplement release, territory adjustment, and energy use persevere. Supportable hydroponics rehearses include nonstop endeavors to relieve natural effects and advance asset use.

Cost of Innovation:

Executing progressed hydroponics innovations, like RAS, can include high starting expenses. For limited scope ranchers or those in creating areas, the moderateness and openness of innovation become huge difficulties. Finding savvy arrangements that offset innovation reception with financial plausibility is urgent.

Market Acknowledgment and Shopper Discernment:

The acknowledgment of hydroponics items by shoppers is impacted by elements like taste, quality, and impression of manageability. Building shopper trust and advancing the advantages of capably cultivated lobster are fundamental for market acknowledgment.

III. Future Possibilities and End:

Coordination of Hydroponics and Preservation:

The fate of lobster hydroponics lies in its mix with protection endeavors. Reasonable hydroponics practices can supplement wild reaps and add to the protection of regular lobster populaces. Laying out hydroponics as a protection instrument includes research, cooperation with administrative bodies, and public mindfulness drives.

Development in Shut Circle Frameworks:

Headways in shut circle hydroponics frameworks, including RAS, hold guarantee for what's in store. Development in innovation, robotization, and energy proficiency can make these frameworks more open and financially suitable for a more extensive scope of aquaculturists. Shut circle frameworks add to maintainability by diminishing water utilization and limiting natural effect.

Local area Commitment and Instruction:

The progress of lobster hydroponics relies upon the help and comprehension of nearby networks. Drawing in networks through instructive projects, straightforward correspondence, and cooperative drives encourages a feeling of shared liability. Informed people group are bound to help supportable hydroponics rehearses.

Worldwide Coordinated effort in Exploration and Guideline:

Tending to difficulties in lobster hydroponics requires worldwide coordinated effort. Scientists, aquaculturists, and administrative bodies should cooperate to share information, best practices, and mechanical advancements. Laying out global norms for capable hydroponics adds to the maintainable advancement of the business.

Consolidating Round Economy Standards:

The reception of round economy standards in hydroponics can upgrade supportability. This includes limiting waste, reusing results, and making shut circle frameworks where sources of info are streamlined. Applying roundabout economy standards to lobster hydroponics lines up with more extensive ecological protection objectives.

Mechanical Advances in Sickness The executives:

Future exploration ought to zero in on creating trend setting innovations for sickness avoidance and the board in lobster hydroponics. This incorporates hereditary procedures for rearing sickness safe strains, quick analytic apparatuses, and accuracy medication draws near. Mechanical advancement in illness the board improves the versatility of hydroponics activities.

Administrative Help for Feasible Practices:

States and administrative bodies assume a urgent part in supporting economical hydroponics rehearses. Laying out clear rules, boosting harmless to the ecosystem advancements, and offering monetary help to limited scope ranchers add to the general progress of lobster hydroponics.

7.1 Overview of European Lobster aquaculture practices

Hydroponics, the controlled development of oceanic living beings, has arisen as a vital participant in satisfying the rising worldwide need for fish. With regards to Europe, where the European Lobster (Homarus gammarus) holds social and financial importance, lobster hydroponics has gotten some forward momentum as a practical option in contrast to wild reaps. This complete outline investigates the set of experiences, current practices, difficulties, and future possibilities of European lobster hydroponics.

II. Authentic Setting: From Wild Collects to Hydroponics Developments

Customary Lobster Fisheries:

The European Lobster has for some time been an objective for conventional fisheries along the shorelines of Europe. Throughout the long term, the interest for lobster has developed, prompting worries about overfishing and the supportability of wild populaces. Customary gathering strategies, including lobster pots and traps, have been the essential method for getting lobsters in European waters.

Early Endeavors at Lobster Hydroponics:

The possibility of lobster hydroponics started to flourish as soon as the twentieth 100 years. Starting endeavors zeroed in on catching and raising adolescent lobsters in controlled conditions, yet challenges connected with endurance rates, sickness the board, and generation obstructed early achievement. These early undertakings laid the basis for the improvement of more modern hydroponics rehearses.

III. Present day Lobster Hydroponics Practices in Europe

Broodstock The board:

Fruitful lobster hydroponics starts with the cautious choice and the executives of broodstock - the grown-up lobsters utilized for proliferation. Broodstock are much of the time kept in specific offices where ecological circumstances emulate their normal territories. Keeping up with hereditary variety, observing wellbeing, and advancing circumstances for proliferation are urgent parts of broodstock the executives.

Incubator Activities:

Lobster incubators assume a vital part in the hydroponics cycle. Controlled conditions inside incubators work with the bring forth of eggs and the raising of hatchlings. Key contemplations in incubation center activities incorporate water quality administration, the improvement of particular feeds, and making conditions that help the effective change from hatchlings to adolescent stages.

Adolescent Raising Frameworks:

Once hatchlings change to adolescent stages, they are moved to raising frameworks that give a reasonable climate to development. These frameworks shift and can incorporate coastal tanks, recycling hydroponics frameworks (RAS), or in-water nooks. Adolescent raising includes observing development rates, streamlining taking care of practices, and establishing conditions that imitate regular territories.

Coastal Hydroponics Frameworks:

Coastal hydroponics frameworks have acquired conspicuousness because of their capacity to control ecological factors and limit the effect on normal environments. These frameworks, including recycling hydroponics frameworks, include land-based offices where lobsters are developed in controlled conditions. Inland hydroponics lessens the gamble of illness transmission, considers all year creation, and adds to supportability.

In-Water Fenced in areas:

In-water nooks, for example, ocean pens or enclosures, are sent in beach front waters to raise lobsters right at home. These nooks give a semi-controlled setting that takes into consideration normal ways of behaving, including tunneling and rummaging. In-water frameworks present open doors for coordinating hydroponics with marine protection endeavors and utilizing normal assets.

Taking care of and Nourishment:

Growing healthfully adjusted takes care of is a basic part of lobster hydroponics. Lobsters are omnivorous, and their eating regimens normally incorporate a mix of marine-based proteins, grains, and other fundamental supplements. Research keeps on zeroing in on improving feed plans to upgrade development rates, propagation, and generally speaking wellbeing in hydroponics settings.

IV. Challenges in European Lobster Hydroponics: Exploring the Amphibian Labyrinth

Infection The board:

Sickness episodes represent a critical danger to lobster hydroponics. Bacterial contaminations, parasitic pervasions, and shell illnesses can influence the wellbeing and endurance of refined lobsters. Illness the board procedures include biosecurity measures, wellbeing observing, and progressing exploration to foster antibodies or medicines.

Hereditary Variety Concerns:

Keeping up with hereditary variety is vital for the drawn out maintainability of lobster hydroponics. In shut frameworks or limited scope tasks, there is a gamble of decreased hereditary variety because of inbreeding. Particular rearing projects that focus on hereditary variety and advantageous characteristics are fundamental for the versatility and flexibility of refined lobster populaces.

Natural Effect:

In spite of endeavors to limit natural effect, hydroponics tasks can in any case impact nearby environments. Supplement release, natural surroundings adjustment, and the getaway of refined people are among the ecological worries related with lobster hydroponics. Manageable practices include nonstop endeavors to alleviate these effects and upgrade asset use.

Administrative Structures:

The advancement of administrative systems for lobster hydroponics shifts across European nations. Conflicting guidelines can present difficulties for the business, influencing variables like site determination, grants, and functional principles. Laying out clear and normalized guidelines is essential for cultivating a steady climate for lobster hydroponics.

V. Future Possibilities: Exploring Towards Maintainable Development

Mechanical Developments:

The eventual fate of European lobster hydroponics is intently attached to mechanical developments. Propels in water quality observing, robotized taking care of frameworks, hereditary advances, and illness location apparatuses will add to the proficiency and maintainability of lobster cultivating. These advancements mean to address existing difficulties and hoist hydroponics rehearses.

Coordinated Multi-Trophic Hydroponics (IMTA):

The idea of Coordinated Multi-Trophic Hydroponics (IMTA) includes developing different species in vicinity to make a decent biological system. Joining lobster cultivating with other viable species, for example, ocean growth or channel taking care of shellfish, can improve supplement cycling, lessen natural effect, and make cooperative energies between hydroponics rehearses.

Particular Rearing for Wanted Characteristics:

Progressing research in particular reproducing expects to improve positive characteristics in refined lobsters. Specific reproducing projects can zero in on qualities, for example, development rates, sickness opposition, and temperature resilience. Rearing for explicit characteristics adds to the improvement of strong and versatile lobster populaces.

Cooperative Exploration Drives:

Cooperation between specialists, industry partners, and legislative bodies is fundamental for driving the economical development of lobster hydroponics. Joint examination drives can address key difficulties, share best practices, and add to the improvement of normalized rules. Cooperative endeavors support the business' flexibility and versatility.

Public Mindfulness and Purchaser Instruction:

Building public mindfulness and teaching purchasers about the advantages of capably cultivated lobster is vital for the business' prosperity. Straightforward correspondence about hydroponics rehearses, natural stewardship, and the job of hydroponics in satisfying fish need encourages customer trust and acknowledgment.

VI. Contextual investigations: European Lobster Hydroponics Examples of overcoming adversity

Norway:

Norway has been at the very front of lobster hydroponics innovative work. The country's hydroponics industry has effectively incorporated lobster cultivating into its assorted portfolio. Research foundations and industry accomplices work together on projects pointed toward improving incubator methods, illness the board, and feasible cultivating rehearses.

Scotland:

Scotland, with its broad shoreline and rich marine assets, has likewise seen development in lobster hydroponics drives. Coastal hydroponics frameworks, including recycling hydroponics frameworks, have been carried out to raise lobsters in controlled conditions. These frameworks add to nearby economies and line up with Scotland's obligation to maintainable hydroponics rehearses.

Sweden:

Sweden has embraced in-water walled in areas as a feature of its lobster hydroponics system. By using normal seaside conditions, Sweden means to consolidate hydroponics with marine protection endeavors. The methodology includes cautious site determination, checking ecological effects, and drawing in neighborhood networks in reasonable hydroponics rehearses.

VII. Supporting Lobster Hydroponics for People in the future

European lobster hydroponics remains at the crossing point of custom and development, offering a pathway to manageable fish creation. As the business explores difficulties and embraces mechanical progressions, the development of this famous shellfish can possibly be a leader for dependable hydroponics in Europe.

The excursion from wild collects to present day hydroponics rehearses mirrors a promise to protecting marine environments, supporting seaside networks, and satisfying the needs of a developing populace. With progressing research, cooperative drives, and a common vision of manageable development, European lobster hydroponics can keep on flourishing, guaranteeing a tradition of overflow for people in the future.

7.2 Advantages, challenges, and sustainable aquaculture

Hydroponics, the cultivating of oceanic life forms, has turned into a vital part of worldwide food creation. As the total populace keeps on developing, there is a rising interest for fish, and hydroponics offers a promising answer for satisfy this need. Be that as it may, the quick development of hydroponics has raised worries about natural effects, sickness the board, and social ramifications. This far reaching investigation digs into the benefits, challenges, and the basic of manageable hydroponics.

II. Benefits of Hydroponics: Fulfilling Worldwide Needs with Dependable Practices

Expanded Fish Creation:

One of the essential benefits of hydroponics is its ability to increment fish creation. As wild fisheries face overexploitation and consumption, hydroponics gives a dependable wellspring of fish and shellfish to fulfill the developing need for protein-rich food.

Decreased Strain on Wild Fisheries:

Hydroponics eases the strain on wild fisheries, permitting regular populaces to recuperate and keep up with natural equilibrium. By giving an elective wellspring of fish, hydroponics adds to the protection of marine environments.

Financial Development and Occupation Creation:

The extension of hydroponics has critical financial ramifications, especially in seaside districts and non-industrial nations. Hydroponics tasks set out business open doors and animate financial development, supporting occupations and adding to neediness easing.

Variety of Species:

Hydroponics incorporates a great many animal varieties, from fish and shrimp to mollusks and kelp. This variety considers the development of species with fluctuating natural and dietary qualities, advancing a stronger and versatile food creation framework.

Controlled Natural Circumstances:

Hydroponics empowers the control of natural circumstances, advancing elements like water quality, temperature, and supplement levels. This control upgrades the productivity of creation, further develops development rates, and diminishes the gamble of infection episodes.

All year Accessibility:

Dissimilar to wild fisheries, which are dependent upon occasional varieties and changes, hydroponics gives a reliable and all year supply of fish. This dependability in accessibility tends to the difficulties of irregularity and upgrades food security.

Mechanical Progressions:

Progressions in hydroponics advances, including recycling hydroponics frameworks (RAS), mechanized taking care of, and hereditary improvement, add to expanded proficiency and manageability. These advancements further develop asset use, decrease ecological effect, and improve in general efficiency.

III. Challenges in Hydroponics: Exploring Complex Waters

Sickness The board:

Sickness flare-ups represent a huge test in hydroponics, influencing both finfish and shellfish. High stocking densities and nearness in hydroponics frameworks can work with the spread of microbes. Compelling infection the executives techniques, including biosecurity measures and immunization programs, are fundamental.

Ecological Effect:

Hydroponics tasks can have ecological results, including supplement release, environment debasement, and the potential for hereditary communications with wild populaces. Tending to these effects requires manageable practices, cautious site choice, and progressing checking.

Feed Reliance:

The dependence on outside feed, frequently obtained from wild-got fish, has raised worries about the manageability of hydroponics. Creating elective and maintainable feed sources, for example, plant-based proteins or bug based takes care of, is pivotal for lessening the business' effect on wild fisheries.

Hereditary Collaborations:

Escapees from hydroponics offices, whether deliberate or inadvertent, can interbreed with wild populaces, prompting hereditary collaborations. Keeping up with hereditary respectability in wild populaces is imperative for protecting neighborhood transformations and forestalling potentially negative side-effects.

Social and Financial Variations:

The advantages of hydroponics are not generally appropriated impartially. Now and again, enormous scope tasks might prompt social and monetary abberations, affecting nearby networks, limited scope ranchers, and customary fishers. Economical hydroponics practices ought to focus on comprehensive and socially mindful methodologies.

Administrative Difficulties:

The administrative systems for hydroponics change universally and may introduce difficulties in guaranteeing steady norms. Successful guidelines ought to address ecological worries, advance dependable practices, and backing the drawn out maintainability of the business.

IV. Manageable Hydroponics: Adjusting Monetary, Natural, and Social Aspects

Eco-Affirmations and Guidelines:

Eco-affirmations, for example, those given by associations like the Hydroponics Stewardship Chamber (ASC) and the Best Hydroponics Practices (BAP), set guidelines for earth and socially dependable hydroponics. Adherence to these confirmations means a guarantee to manageability and capable practices.

Incorporated Multi-Trophic Hydroponics (IMTA):

IMTA is an imaginative methodology that includes developing various species in closeness to make a decent biological system. Joining fish, shellfish, and kelp can improve supplement cycling, lessen natural effects, and advance a more manageable and versatile hydroponics framework.

Shut Circle Frameworks:

Shut circle hydroponics frameworks, like RAS, limit water trade and improve asset use. These frameworks improve command over natural circumstances, diminish the gamble of sickness transmission, and add to the general maintainability of hydroponics tasks.

Elective Feeds:

Creating and embracing elective and supportable feeds is a vital technique for decreasing the business' dependence on wild-gotten fish. Plant-based proteins, green growth, and bug based takes care of are among the choices being investigated to give a healthfully adjusted diet to cultivated species.

Local area Commitment and Social Obligation:

Supportable hydroponics includes connecting with neighborhood networks, regarding conventional information, and advancing social obligation. Cooperative methodologies that focus on local area prosperity, comprehensive direction, and fair work rehearses add to the general maintainability of the hydroponics area.

Examination and Development:

Progressing exploration and development are fundamental for tending to the difficulties in hydroponics. Progresses in hereditary qualities, sickness the executives, and hydroponics advancements add to additional reasonable practices. Research drives ought to focus on arrangements that balance financial, natural, and social aspects.

V. Contextual investigations: Models of Supportable Hydroponics Practices

Norwegian Salmon Cultivating:

Norway, a worldwide forerunner in salmon hydroponics, has carried out supportable practices like rigid guidelines, RAS advances, and eco-certificates. These actions add to the business' standing for mindful hydroponics and backing the protection of wild salmon populaces.

Vietnamese Pangasius Cultivating:

The pangasius business in Vietnam has gained ground in maintainability through the reception of mindful cultivating works on, including the utilization of affirmed takes care of, productive water the executives, and local area commitment. This area exhibits the potential for positive natural and social effects through reasonable hydroponics.

Shrimp Cultivating in Ecuador:

Shrimp cultivating in Ecuador confronted difficulties connected with ecological effect and illness episodes. Through the reception of better administration rehearses, natural confirmation, and endeavors to diminish reliance on wild-gotten feed, the business has gained ground toward more maintainable and eco-accommodating shrimp cultivating.

VI. Future Headings: Exploring Towards a Blue Upheaval 2.0

Round Economy Standards:

Applying round economy standards to hydroponics includes limiting waste, reusing results, and making shut circle frameworks. This approach lines up with more extensive supportability objectives and adds to asset effectiveness in hydroponics activities.

Accuracy Hydroponics:

Accuracy hydroponics use innovation, information examination, and mechanization to streamline creation effectiveness and asset use. Ongoing checking of natural circumstances, fish conduct, and feed utilization takes into consideration designated intercessions, decreasing the environmental impression of hydroponics.

Advancements in Sea-going Wellbeing:

Headways in oceanic wellbeing the board, including the improvement of immunizations, sickness safe strains, and fast demonstrative devices, will assume a significant part in moderating illness challenges in hydroponics. These developments add to the business' versatility and manageability.

Hydroponics Combination:

Coordinating hydroponics with aqua-farming in hydroponics frameworks makes harmonious connections among fish and plants. Fish squander gives supplements to establish development, and plants help channel and refine the water. Hydroponics frameworks epitomize an all encompassing and asset proficient way to deal with maintainable food creation.

Worldwide Cooperation for Guidelines:

Reinforcing worldwide joint effort for the turn of events and reception of normal principles in hydroponics is fundamental. A bound together way to deal with manageability principles, guidelines, and certificates can advance consistency and straightforwardness, supporting capable practices across borders.

Interest in Limited scope and Comprehensive Hydroponics:

Perceiving the significance of limited scope and comprehensive hydroponics is pivotal for advancing manageability. Supporting neighborhood and customary hydroponics works on, engaging limited scope ranchers, and guaranteeing fair market access add to the social and financial elements of supportability.

7.3 Summary of key findings, implications, and future directions

As we set out on an exhaustive excursion through the immense field of information incorporating different points, the rundown unites key discoveries, investigates their suggestions, and graphs a course toward future headings. From scientific classification and science to manageable hydroponics and then some, the blend of experiences assembled discloses an embroidery of understanding that shapes our view of the normal world and the difficulties and open doors it presents.

II. Scientific categorization, Science, and Life Cycle: Uncovering the Secrets of Nature

In the investigation of scientific categorization, the order of living creatures, key discoveries enlighten the complexities of various leveled frameworks utilized by researcher to comprehend and sort life. Understanding scientific classification fills in as an establishment for diving into the science of creatures, disentangling the secrets of their design, capability, and natural jobs. A focus on life cycles gives bits of knowledge into the perplexing dance of birth, development, proliferation, and demise, fundamental components in the propagation of life on The planet.

III. Ordered Arrangement and Key Attributes: Interpreting Nature's Diagram

The excursion into ordered characterization develops with an accentuation on key attributes that characterize and recognize species. From minute living beings to transcending trees, the order gives a guide to figuring out biodiversity. Suggestions reach out to preservation endeavors, as the information on key attributes illuminates techniques for safeguarding and protecting the different cluster of life on our planet.

IV. Life Cycle Stages and Formative Achievements: The Ensemble of Development

Life cycle stages and formative achievements coordinate the ensemble of development across the natural range. Understanding these stages is significant for unwinding the complexities of development, variation, and biological collaborations. From the little seeds of plants to the transformation of bugs and the development of well evolved creatures, every life cycle stage holds importance in forming the multifaceted snare of life.

V. Regenerative Way of behaving and Systems: Nature's Dance of Creation

In the domain of regenerative way of behaving and systems, the dance of creation unfurls. From romance ceremonies and mating ways of behaving to the different methodologies utilized by creatures to guarantee the endurance of their hereditary heritage, this investigation dives into the entrancing universe of proliferation. Key discoveries highlight the variety of conceptive procedures across species, each finely tuned to the particular biological specialties they possess.

VI. Dissemination, Environment, and Biology: Uncovering Nature's Geographic Embroidery

The geographic reach and environments of life forms paint a striking embroidery of biodiversity. Understanding conveyance designs, living space inclinations, and environmental associations give bits of knowledge into the fragile equilibrium that supports biological systems. From the frigid territories of the Icy to the lavish rainforests and energetic coral reefs, the investigation of circulation, natural surroundings, and environment disentangles the interconnectedness of life across the globe.

VII. Geographic Reach and Territories in Atlantic Waters: Exploring the Atlantic Chasm

An emphasis on the Atlantic Waters dives into the particular geographic reach and territories that characterize this huge marine scope. From the cool flows of the North Atlantic to the warm subtropical waters, the Atlantic Sea harbors a different cluster of marine life. Investigating the one of a kind variations of organic entities to these living spaces and understanding the environmental elements of the Atlantic Waters gives a nuanced viewpoint on the difficulties and open doors introduced by this far reaching marine domain.

VIII. Ecological Necessities and Elements Impacting Appropriation: Adjusting Nature's Condition

The appropriation of species is complicatedly connected to their ecological necessities. Grasping the elements that impact dissemination, from environment and temperature to geology and asset accessibility, reveals insight into the sensitive equilibrium that administers the spatial plan of life. Suggestions reach out to preservation techniques, as the effect of ecological changes on dissemination designs turns into a point of convergence for moderating dangers to biodiversity.

IX. Taking care of Propensities, Dietary Inclinations, and Biological Connections: The Culinary Accounts of Nature

Taking care of propensities and dietary inclinations uncover the culinary narratives of nature, investigating the different manners by which organic entities get food. From herbivores brushing on vegetation to carnivores taking part in predation, the investigation of taking care of propensities gives bits of knowledge into natural jobs and connections. Understanding the complexities of food networks and trophic elements illuminates preservation endeavors and environment the board.

X. Fisheries and Business Significance: Gathering the Sea's Abundance

The human relationship with the sea-going domain becomes the dominant focal point in the investigation of fisheries and business significance. Fishing, a training imbued in mankind's set of experiences, has developed into a worldwide industry that gives food and financial vocations. The business significance of fisheries stretches out past neighborhood networks, impacting worldwide business sectors and exchange. Nonetheless, the difficulties of overfishing, environment debasement, and bycatch highlight the requirement for economical fisheries the executives.

XI. Verifiable Viewpoint of European Lobster Fisheries: A Narrative of Harvests

The authentic point of view of European Lobster fisheries follows the development of human connections with this notorious shellfish. From conventional harvests to the difficulties presented by expanded request, overfishing, and natural changes, the account mirrors the perplexing connection among social orders and marine assets. Examples from history illuminate contemporary ways to deal with lobster fisheries the board and preservation.

XII. Financial Importance and Business Worth: Lobsters as Monetary Resources

The monetary importance and business worth of lobsters reach out past their culinary allure. As important items in worldwide business sectors, lobsters contribute altogether to the economies of locales with dynamic fisheries. Looking at the financial aspects includes understanding business sector patterns, exchange elements, and the job of lobster fisheries in supporting occupations and beach front networks.

XIII. Feasible Fisheries The board Works on: Sustaining the Blue Heritage

Reasonable fisheries the executives rehearses arise as a foundation for saving marine assets. From share frameworks and stuff guidelines to marine safeguarded regions and local area based administration, a set-up of methodologies means to offset human requirements with environmental maintainability. Best practices in fisheries the executives offer a guide for exploring the intricacies of asset use while shielding the soundness of marine environments.

XIV. Protection Difficulties and Endeavors: Shielding the Delicate Equilibrium

Protection difficulties and endeavors feature the fragile harmony between human exercises and the safeguarding of biodiversity. Living space misfortune, contamination, environmental change, and intrusive species present dangers to biological systems around the world. Preservation endeavors include a scope of systems, from safeguarded regions and rebuilding ventures to local area commitment and strategy support. The basic of preservation highlights the aggregate liability to steward the planet's regular legacy.

XV. Preservation Status of European Lobster Populaces: Surveying the Strength of a Notorious Animal groups

Evaluating the preservation status of European Lobster populaces gives a preview of the animal types' wellbeing and weakness. From populace evaluations to checking key markers, researchers and preservationists work to measure the effect of human exercises on lobster populaces. Experiences into the preservation status illuminate designated intercessions and strategy measures pointed toward getting the eventual fate of this famous shellfish.

XVI. Dangers to Their Endurance: Exploring Risks in the Marine Domain

Dangers to the endurance of marine species, including the European Lobster, radiate from different sources. Overfishing, natural surroundings corruption, environmental change, and contamination present imposing difficulties to marine biological systems. Distinguishing and tending to these dangers require a complex methodology that incorporates logical exploration, strategy intercessions, and local area commitment.

XVII. Environmental Change Effects and Variations: The Unfurling Show in Changing Oceans

Environmental change creates a long shaded area over the marine domain, impacting temperatures, flows, and biological communications. The effects of environmental change on marine species, including lobsters, require transformations for endurance. From shifts in appropriation examples to changes in regenerative ways of behaving, understanding the natural results of environmental change illuminates methodologies for flexibility and protection.

XVIII. Impact of Environmental Change on Atlantic Waters and Lobster Living spaces: The Dance of Sea and Climate

The impact of environmental change on Atlantic Waters and lobster territories uncovers a mind boggling dance among sea and climate. From increasing ocean temperatures to sea fermentation, the changing environment presents difficulties and valuable open doors for marine life. Understanding the perplexing associations between environment factors and biological reactions guides endeavors to alleviate the effect of environmental change on Atlantic environments.

XIX. Social and Physiological Transformations to Evolving Conditions: The Orchestra of Variation

Organic entities answer changing circumstances with an ensemble of conduct and physiological transformations. From adjusted movement examples to changes in taking care of ways of behaving, the ability to adjust is fundamental for endurance. Investigating these variations gives bits of knowledge into the versatility of species even with ecological change and illuminates preservation methodologies.

XX. Research Strategies and Methods: Opening Nature's Privileged insights

Research strategies and methods act as the way to opening nature's mysteries. From field perceptions and hereditary examinations to remote detecting and displaying, researchers utilize a different tool compartment to investigate the complexities of the normal world. The development of procedures in concentrating on marine life reflects headways in innovation, interdisciplinary joint effort, and an extending comprehension of natural cycles.

XXI. Outline of Philosophies Utilized in Concentrating on European Lobster: From Tides to Innovation

An outline of procedures utilized in concentrating on the European Lobster dives into the particular strategies utilized to unwind the secrets of this notorious scavanger. From mark-recover studies and submerged overviews to hereditary examinations and telemetry, specialists utilize a mix of conventional and state of the art strategies to acquire experiences into the science, conduct, and environment of European Lobsters.

XXII. Mechanical Progressions in Lobster Exploration: Exploring the Advanced Wilderness

Mechanical headways in lobster research drive the field into the advanced boondocks. From submerged robots and satellite following to DNA sequencing and bioinformatics, innovation improves the accuracy and extent of lobster studies. The reconciliation of innovation speeds up the speed of disclosure as well as opens new roads for observing and preservation endeavors.

XXIII. Difficulties and Future Possibilities in Lobster Exploration: Cruising Into the great beyond

Difficulties and future possibilities in lobster research highlight the unique idea of logical request. From addressing information holes and refining strategies to exploring subsidizing requirements, specialists outline a course toward a skyline of disclosure. Cooperative endeavors, interdisciplinary methodologies, and a pledge to information scattering shape the future scene of lobster research.

XXIV. Hydroponics Potential and End: Supporting Manageable Blue Fates

The capability of hydroponics arises as an encouraging sign in gathering the difficulties of food security, ecological supportability, and financial turn of events. From the development of European Lobster to the more extensive setting of economical hydroponics rehearses, the excursion finishes up with a reflection on the possibilities of hydroponics in molding a blue future. Adjusting financial feasibility, ecological stewardship, and social obligation, hydroponics holds the way to supporting practical and versatile food frameworks.

XXV. Outline of European Lobster Hydroponics Works on: Cruising the Waters of Manageability

An outline of European Lobster hydroponics rehearses plunges into the complexities of developing this notorious species. From broodstock the board and incubator tasks to coastal hydroponics frameworks and in-water nooks, the techniques utilized in lobster hydroponics mirror a pledge to manageability. Illustrations from fruitful contextual analyses feature the capability of dependable hydroponics in supporting seaside economies and monitoring marine assets.

XXVI. Benefits, Difficulties, and Reasonable Hydroponics: Making the Blue Upheaval 2.0

Benefits, challenges, and reasonable hydroponics structure the essence of the Blue Upheaval 2.0. From expanded fish creation and monetary development to infection the executives and ecological effect, the story explores the complicated waters of hydroponics. Embracing roundabout economy standards, accuracy hydroponics, and worldwide cooperation, the eventual fate of hydroponics holds the commitment of a tough and reasonable blue boondocks.